ings

"This book i   ls that will take
your sales c

                                                  —Jerry Wilson,

F   *g Franchise Owner,*

                                    ; Millennium Group

This is a trul   cel in sales. The
wisdom in th   orth more than
many compe   Byrd and Larry will
help you to l   most powerfully
persuasive p   in life! Read this
book, use its lessons, and change your life!

—Tom Morris,
Author of Philosophy for Dummies, True Success, The
Art of Achievement, If Aristotle Ran General Motors, *and*
If Harry Potter Ran General Electric

97 Things to Take Your Sales Career to the Next Level

This book is dedicated to the many client friends who have entrusted us to serve their organizations.

97 Things to Take Your Sales Career to the Next Level

Byrd Baggett, CSP
and Larry Cole, Ph.D.

TRADE PAPER
PRESS

Turner Publishing Company

445 Park Avenue, 9th Floor
New York, NY 10022
Phone: (212)710-4338   Fax: (212)710-4339

200 4th Avenue North, Suite 950
Nashville, TN 37219
Phone: (615)255-2665   Fax: (615)255-5081

www.turnerpublishing.com

97 Things to Take Your Sales Career to the Next Level

Copyright © 2010 Byrd Baggett and Larry Cole

Library of Congress Cataloging-in-Publication Data

Baggett, Byrd.
 97 things to take your sales career to the next level / Byrd Baggett and Larry Cole.
    p. cm.
 ISBN 978-1-59652-749-2
1. Selling. 2. Career development. I. Cole, Larry, 1945- II. Title. III. Title: Ninety seven things to take
your sales career to the next level.
 HF5438.25.B268 2010
 658.85--dc22
                          2010034332

Printed in China

10 11 12 13 14 15 16—0 9 8 7 6 5 4 3 2 1

Business Forecast

BUSINESS will continue to go where invited and remain where appreciated.

REPUTATIONS will continue to be made by many acts and lost by one.

PEOPLE will go right on preferring to do business with friends.

PRODUCT KNOWLEDGE will have no substitute. KNOW-HOW will surpass guess-how.

ENTHUSIASM will be as contagious as ever.

PERFORMANCE will continue to outsell promises.

QUALITY will be prized as a precious possession.

TRUST, not tricks, will keep customers loyal.

THE EXTRA MILE will have no traffic jams!

~Anonymous

Contents

Introduction

Is your sales career green and growing or ripe and rotting? To help you answer that question, take the Ripeness Test below, then read and reflect upon the following true story of a sales professional who works in the insurance and financial services industry.

✓ Ripeness Test

Are you green and growing or ripe and rotting?
Please circle the number that best fits you & your current life:

1. 1 ——— ③ ——— 5 ——— 7 ——— 9
   I rarely encourage others / I frequently encourage others

2. 1 ——— 3 ——— 5 ——— ⑦ ——— 9
   I resist change / I adapt well to change

3. 1 ——— 3 ——— 5 ——— ⑦ ——— 9
   I long for the past and the way things used to be / I look forward to the future

4. 1 ——— 3 ——— ⑤ ——— 7 ——— 9
   I am unhappy with my job / I love my job

5. 1 ——— 3 ——— 5 ——— 7 ——— ⑨
   I am unhappy with my significant other / I am happy with my significant other

6. 1 ——— 3 ——— ⑤ ——— 7 ——— 9
   I participate in destructive communication / I participate in healthy, open and constructive communication

7. 1 ——— 3 ——— 5 ——— 7 ——— ⑨
   I am frequently in a bad mood / I am most often in a good mood

8. 1 ——— 3 ——— 5 ——— ⑦ ——— 9
   I frequently say negative things / I rarely say negative things

9. 1 ——— 3 ——— 5 ——— 7 ——— ⑨
   I rarely smile / I frequently smile

10. 1 ——— 3 ——— 5 ——— 7 ——— ⑨
    I prefer being alone / I enjoy being with others

11. 1 ——— 3 ——— 5 ——— 7 ——— ⑨
    I distrust others / I trust others

✓Ripeness Test
Results

_____ **My Ripeness Score**

Compare your score to the following Ripeness Ratings:

Vibrant: 99
Healthy: 77
Fair: 55
Poor: 33
Dangerous: 11

If you're green and growing, congratulations! If you're not, what simple acts of daily discipline do you need to apply to your life?

Eddy's sales journey

Age: *66*
Profession: *Insurance Agent*
2004 Ripeness Test score: *27 – Very unhealthy*
2005 Ripeness Test score: *95 – Passionately engaged*

What did Eddy do to make this remarkable life change? Following is what he had to say about his journey.

Season of Self/Season of Drought

"I had a bad attitude and didn't want to hear anything from management, as I already knew that it was going to be bad. I felt that management had no idea what I was going through and didn't care about me. I started staying away from the office more and more. Why go to work and be miserable? My wife told me she had never seen me this way."

Season of New Growth

To what do you attribute your change?
"I had read enough to know that when you are truly tired of the place you're in, it's time to make a change. After I decided I was not going to retire and walk away with my tail between my legs, I decided I was going to get out of this bad place I was in and

start back to living life and having fun in my business. Once I made this decision, I was receptive to hearing about ways to do this new job."

Season of Significance

What are the symptoms of the reengaged Eddy?

"Wow, life is great! My family life has greatly improved and my business is growing at a fast pace again. In 2005 I had the biggest life premium year ever ($75,000) and qualified for my company's most prestigious performance awards. It's May of 2006 and I have about as much life premium as I did in all of 2005—tell me that attitude doesn't matter!"

Season of New Growth

What did you do to get better?

"True relationships have honesty in them. I asked my management team to honestly assess my strengths and weaknesses. I wanted to know how I could get better."

"I realized that if I wanted better relationships, I had to take the initiative. I needed to take responsibility for myself and not blame others for where I was."

"Once I started taking responsibility and quit blaming others, my failures were fewer and smaller. Due to my 'awakening' I didn't have time to dwell on the negatives, as I had much more positives in my life to tend to."

Eddy's closing comments

"Can you guess that I don't like to listen to agents griping in our meetings? I try to make better the things I can and don't spend time on the things I can't control. I'm 66 years old and have no retirement plans. How big and good can I build this agency? I don't know the answer but I'll have a ball doing it!"

Keys to Eddy's growth

- Started having conversations with clients to

help identify what they needed, what was important to them
- Quit selling and started developing relationships
- Got out of self and into others

SEASONS OF GROWTH™

SEASON OF SELF

SEASON OF DROUGHT

SEASON OF NEW GROWTH

SEASON OF SIGNIFICANCE

It's all about ME

Into self is a very lonely place

You must let go to grow

Being a part of something greater than self

After reading and reflecting on Eddy's story, how do you feel about your sales career? How did you score on the Ripeness Test? Were you green and growing or ripe and rotting? If you were green and growing, congratulations! If you feel your sales career is ripe and rotting, we encourage you to identify the simple acts of daily discipline that are required to add some green to your life. Whatever condition you find your sales career in, the purpose of this simple handbook is to share practical and applicable insights and strategies, some found in chapters ("Things") with descriptive text, and others that are simply insightful quotes. When applied, these insights and strategies will take your sales career to the next level—to the richly rewarding Season of Significance.

Note: Eddy enjoyed a record year of production in 2007, his fortieth year in the business. His business and life are green and growing!

Enjoy the journey to sales excellence,

Byrd Baggett

Larry Cole

The 97 Things

– 1 –
Three steps to change

Want to take your sales career to the next level? Then focus on these three steps to change:

1. Awareness:

You learn something new but you haven't changed.

2. Intention:

You're excited about applying what you've learned, but your intentions have yet to change anything.

3. Action:

Change occurs when you apply those simple acts of daily discipline that are required to bring alive what you've learned.

Recommendation

As you read and reflect on the 97 Things (including this one) that can take your sales career to the next level, we recommend that you think on these three steps to change and ask yourself the following question after reading each entry: "What new behavior did I learn that I can apply to take my sales career to the next level?" Write these new behaviors down, as we will return to your list at the end of the book.

– 2 –
Seven-step process to change

We're introducing 97 ideas in this book for you to promote your sales career. With so many ideas, we would be remiss not to tell you how to change your behavior. This chapter is longer than others because it is crucial that you understand the basic concepts associated with the change process in order for you to manage the energy systems inherent in the personal change process.

Yes, there are two energy systems. You are either changing and moving forward to acquire a new behavior, or the lure of the comfort zone is keeping you locked in an existing rut. You need to manage the energy systems to continue walking down the path labeled change.

1. Accept responsibility

It is critical that you accept responsibility for creating the person you are today and understanding that you are the only person who can change you. It's a matter of choice. You can blame other people for who you are today, but blaming is not going to get you far.

Do you want to maximize your personal potential? How successful do you want to be as a salesperson? The answers to these questions will help determine whether you are willing to accept the responsibility to *change.*

2. Recognize the need

Recognizing the need to change is based on the intensity of the disadvantages associated with the person you are today. You function in a comfort zone, and your existing behaviors have both advantages and disadvantages. The intensity of the energy associated with your current behavior's

disadvantages must exceed the intensity of the
energy associated with the advantages of remaining
as you are. In other words, you must make the
decision, *"I can no longer remain as is."*

3. Know your desired behavior

Most of the ideas in this book include suggested
behavioral blueprints to integrate into your day-to-
day life. Knowing where you want to go and how
to get there are essential to being able to successfully change. As the cliché states, if you don't know
where you want to go, anywhere will do, and that
principle is certainly not going to improve your sales
career.

4. Be willing to change

Another factor is being introduced into the
change formula. You've probably had the experience
of purchasing an item that exceeded your budget,
but you bought it anyway—it literally sucked the

money right out of your pocket! Again, there are going to be advantages and disadvantages associated with the new behavior listed in Step 3. You want the advantages of this behavior—the willingness to change—to have such a strong magnetic appeal that it literally pulls you to overcome the disadvantages of the energy source encouraging you to remain as is. You want to make the decision, *"Remaining as is is no option, and I must become the person described in Step 3!"*

5. Have a personal image

Do you see yourself engaging the behavior listed in Step 3? The importance of seeing yourself practice this behavior is that your body follows your eyes. For example, Larry does not see himself picking up snakes. Do you think he will? No! Enough said.

6. Practice the change

You have three opportunities to practice the change. One is through visual imagery. This opportunity is available to you at any time. Second is through being in a classroom or role-playing with a trainer or friend. Third is simply through practicing every day, all day long. Every prospect you talk to is another practice session. Right now, you are either practicing these behaviors to improve your performance, or you're practicing those behaviors that are interfering with your progress. Again, it's your choice. But we want you to make a good choice.

As a salesperson, do you consider resistance as a positive event or a negative one? Remember the pleasure-pain principle—we're attracted to pleasure and tempted to avoid pain. Thus, if you perceive resistance as a negative event, you're tempted to avoid engaging in the behavior—resistance—that results in pain. Research even shows a neurological basis for this resistance. Realize, however, that you're going to experience resistance to your personal change, as change requires hard work, time, and overcoming fears. You want to perceive these as your stepping-stones to success; therefore, you should perceive resistance as a positive event.

We've listed two positive energy sources for promoting change in steps 2 and 4. Resistance can reverse the positive energy and convince you to look back at the comfort of the comfort zone. When these diametrically opposed energy sources clash, the stronger may win. You're in a danger zone; you can continue changing, or you can quit. As Norman Vincent Peale said, "We quit when we accept the image of defeat." Now is the time to keep your eyes locked onto the person you want to become, taking advantage of the fact that your body follows your eyes.

There are daily activities to help you change. Keep in mind that you want to saturate your daily existence with becoming the new person. The more you practice, the faster you change. Following are some activities for your consideration.

    A. Focus on a limited number of behaviors. Select a couple behaviors to focus on from the 96 that we offer in this book.

    B. Begin the day thinking about the person you're going to be today. World-class performers use every practice session as an opportunity to improve a specific element of their performance. You want to do the same. Review the reasons that remaining the same is no option and that you must be the person you listed in Step 3. Start every day focused on the behaviors you're improving.

    C. Focus on your can-do attitude. For example, focus on what's left, not what's lost, and count five good things before you earn the right to one worry. Finally, instead of thinking "I have to," think "I get to."

    D. Whenever you're tempted to regress and use your old behavior, tell yourself to stop and think. Then ask, "Do I want to make a good choice or a bad choice?" Psychologically, you want to make a good choice, which is to continue using the new behavior.

E. Act as if you are already the person you are working to be. Over time, acting "as if" will become easier.

F. There may be times when you have to review the disadvantages associated with being your old self and the advantages of being the person you've listed in Step 3. Pep talks can be very beneficial.

G. Spend at least fifteen minutes each day reading a good book that lifts your spirits. A good book is a great teacher.

7. Feedback

Feedback is crucial for long-term behavior change. I hope that your sales manager will provide feedback on your progress. You may not see an immediate increase in your sales production, but at the end of the day, evaluate the success made on that particular day and look for something good about which you can pat yourself on the back. If the day did not progress as you would have liked, reflect on the following words taken from Catherine Ponder's book *The Dynamic Laws of Prosperity:* "Failure is success trying to be born in another way."

Now you know how to change your behavior. No excuses!

— 3 —

You must let go to grow

What bad behaviors are keeping you from taking your sales career to the next level? Asking the following question may help: "What two behaviors are keeping me from being a better sales professional?" These are the behaviors that you need to let go to grow.

— 4 —

Greatness takes time to grow

Once the Chinese bamboo plant is planted (your new behaviors), there is no visible growth for up to five years, even under the most ideal conditions. Then, as if by magic, it suddenly begins growing at the rate of nearly 2.5 feet per day, reaching as high as ninety feet within six weeks!

What is Mother Nature trying to tell us? Greatness takes time to grow, and we must be patient once we plant our new behavior seeds.

‑ 5 ‑
2/24/90 Principle

You know the proverbial saying that to eat an elephant, you take one bite at a time. Completing all the responsibilities of being a high-performing salesperson can be as daunting as the "eating the elephant" assignment. As you ponder the mountain of work, you'll notice that energy drains from your body. It's like a slow leak in the water jug. Eventually, the jug will become dry.

Sometimes you need a kick-start to take the first bite of the elephant, and that's where the 2/24/90 Principle ™ can be of assistance. This principle states that you need to discover two behaviors within the next twenty-four hours that will kick-start your sales career. Then focus on living these new behaviors consistently for the next ninety days. We've already discussed the requirement to build neural highways to support the behavior change. This ninety-day practice period can help jump-start the long-term change process. One thing is for certain: the ninety-first time you complete these two behaviors will be easier than the first time!

May we suggest a good place to start? Let's start each day with positive energy and expectations. We'll be teaching you seven behaviors to put more optimism in your life, but in case that's too big of a bite to take, focus on a couple steps of that plan for the next ninety days. First, each night before going to sleep, think about one good reason you want to wake up in the morning. Second, wake up fifteen to thirty minutes earlier and do something that you truly enjoy. Perhaps it's reading something motivational to start your day. Another good motivating exercise is to spend a few minutes journaling, or putting your thoughts and feelings in writing. Start each day with a mini-vacation.

After ninety days, you can add two more behaviors. You can actually start a personal change system to focus on improving two behaviors every ninety days. Developing the habit to continually improve your performance can be a good thing for you, your family, and your career.

Values are the roots that determine the fruit

As we nonchalantly enjoy eating our favorite fruit, we seldom think about all the work the plant does to help us enjoy eating healthy. As you know, roots are vital to the success of every plant. Without roots soaking up necessary nutrients and water, the plant dies, and there is no fruit. The plant is alive, but it doesn't have the capability to think or feel as we do; therefore, it's easy to take the critical functions of the root for granted.

Likewise, we take our root structure for granted. Like the plant's root structure, our values determine the person others see. Most of us quietly acquired our root structure over the course of our lives. We seldom stop to ponder, *What are my values telling my prospects and clients about me? Would I like to buy from me?*

The truth of the matter is that successful selling is determined by your capability to establish relationships, a capability determined by your personal values. In reality, you make your personal values, and then they make you.

We encourage you to complete an exercise. First, generate a comprehensive list of your personal values, or visit the Web to purchase a set of values cards—there are numerous options available (www.truegrowthassociates.com and www.sustainable-employee-motivation.com). Second, place your lists into two categories, those most important to you and those least important to you. Third is the most difficult assignment: from your list of most important values, select the seven that are critical for you, the values that you consider most important.

How good do you want to be? Do you want to grow your sales career to the next level? We ask you these questions because your answers will determine whether you take this values exercise to the next level. If you want to be the best version of yourself, then give your comprehensive list to several of your work associates and clients. Ask them to sort your answers into two categories—those most like you, and those least like you. Then ask them to identify the seven that are the most like you. Finally, create a composite of this information and compare it to the list that you created. What does it tell you? Do others see you as you want to be seen?

Successful salespeople know who they are. They know the reputation they create with their prospects and clients. Do yourself a favor—complete this exercise.

― 7 ―
Trust is the lifeblood of relationships

Trust is a key ingredient in the success of the sales relationship because your prospects like to buy from people they trust. You want to ensure that trust is in your sales tool kit.

The importance of trust creates an interesting dilemma. That is, people agree that trust is the lifeblood of relationships, but many people struggle with knowing the behaviors they must practice to be a trusting person. You would think that because trust is so important that our educational or workplace learning experiences would have taught us how to be trustworthy. Tragically, that's not the case.

We've got good news for you. Listed below are essential behaviors for you to adhere to in order to be a trustworthy salesperson.

Be dependable

When you make a commitment to a prospect or client, make sure to meet or exceed that commitment. You want to be the person who under-promises and over-delivers. In those *rare* occasions when you can't keep your commitments—for whatever reason—tell your prospect or customer immediately. You may be tempted to delay being a messenger of bad news, but don't yield to the temptation. Face your fear and do it anyway. Now!

Be competent

It is imperative to have current product knowledge and appear confident. Your prospects and customers feel secure that you can fulfill their needs when they think that you know what you're talking about. When competent people don't know the answer to a question, they admit it and make a commitment to find the answer and get back with the client. Then be dependable—get back with the client when you said you would.

There are times when you won't feel as confident as you would like. In these instances, act as if you are confident. When such instances occur, remember that your body is telling you to learn something. Learn it—you do that by practicing, practicing, and practicing some more.

Keep confidences

This should go without saying. When you talk about other customers, you send the message that you will talk about "me" to other customers. That's a trust-breaker!

Keep customers informed

Have you noticed that the figments of our imaginations quickly become our realities? This is particularly true when our minds do not have the facts about a situation. When that happens, our minds go into overdrive and generate false assumptions. You need to be aware that when you do not keep prospects and customers informed of the facts, their minds will generate their own facts. Additionally, the feeling of not being informed with the facts erodes trust. The message is clear: keep prospects and customers informed with needed information.

Now that you've got the essentials, it's up to you to put these behaviors to work.

– 8 –

Trust, once lost, is almost impossible to regain.

Customers love humility

You want your ego to be a strength, not your Achilles' heel.

In their best-selling book *Egonomics: What Makes Ego Our Greatest Asset (or Most Expensive Liability),* authors David Marcum and Steven Smith offer one of the better discussions about humility. These authors place ego on a continuum with humility as the desired behavior, as illustrated in the following figure.

Ego Empty	HUMILITY	Egotistical
Lack of self-confidence	Intelligent	Overconfident
Self-esteem	Self-respect Genuine confidence	Arrogant

As with many psychological characteristics, one wonders how genetics and one's learning history influence the adult ego. Does your ego control you, or are you in control of your ego? In reality, you want to control the ego instead of it controlling you.

Marcum and Smith propose that being humble is the ideal state. It would be nice if a "healthy dose of humility" was genetically "fixed," but that appears not to be the case. Instead, you must learn to be humble, and that produces another challenge: What must you learn to become more humble?

Definitions offered through a variety of resource materials speak in terms of "not being arrogant" or "not being boastful." How can you "not be something?" To "not" be something, you must "be" something. Many reference books recommend being "modest," "unpretentious," and "respectful," to name a few. Marcum and Smith offer the following definition: "Humility is intelligent self-respect that keeps us from thinking too much or too little of ourselves. It reminds us how far we have come while at the same time helping us see how far short we are of what we can be."

These authors provide three overriding behavioral characteristics that are illustrated in the following figure.

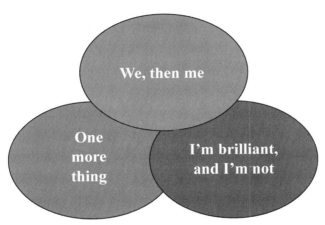

1. "We, then me"

Be the person who puts your prospect first, company second, and "you" third. That means you are willing to sacrifice yourself for the prospect in the absence of an immediate or apparent return to you.

2. "I'm brilliant, and I'm not"

These authors speak to the duality feature of being humble—for example, you are as comfortable allowing the prospect to lead the conversation as you are in leading it. Examples of other duality features include being competitive, flexible, easygoing, and patient, to name a few.

3. "One more thing"

Through your competence, you recognize your incompetence. You are a work in progress. In the words of Matthew Kelly, author of *The Rhythm of Life: Living Every Day with Passion and Purpose,* "you are becoming the best version of yourself."

Customers are going to love your humility, and you will also.

— 10 —
Listen, listen, listen, and listen some more

Listening presents an interesting dilemma for the assertive salesperson who likes to talk. Actually, assertiveness is an important behavioral characteristic for a salesperson for many reasons, including being a self-starter. Fortunately or unfortunately, whichever the case may be, assertiveness is often expressed through one's mouth. Consequently, it's easy to forget why you have two ears and only one mouth!

It's important to show your prospect that they're important. There is an easy process for you to do that. First, ask questions to secure input. Not only are you asking in order to learn about the prospect's needs, but psychologically, you are also showing the prospect that they're important. That's a critical message to send.

Second—you guessed it—listen to understand the client's perspective. Another excellent technique to use is paraphrasing, e.g., *"Let me repeat what I've heard, just to be certain that I understand what you've said."* Always repeat the first step of asking more questions to clarify. Asking questions can also help you identify objections. That is, if you anticipate what an objection might be, ask the prospect questions that will allow them to address it. For example, *"Would you agree that we've got the pricing structured to maximize the return on your financial investment?"* Another example might be, *"Are there any other concerns or issues that I need to be aware of as I finalize the proposal for you?"* Then listen. Prospects often tell you how to sell them if you listen to them.

While you're having this critical conversation, also listen to your body. Frequently spoken words from prospects can elicit emotional responses from you that may not be conducive to a selling relationship. You want to be aware of such emotional responses before they negatively impact the words emerging from your mouth. Sometimes assertive people talk before they think. That's not necessarily a good thing! Once aware of this dynamic, you can control your reactions by telling yourself to remain calm, relaxed, and in control.

Third is showing the prospect that you've listened and understand by paraphrasing how their input helped you to identify what you are selling them. For example, *"Based on what I'm hearing you say, you are really interested in me assisting you with . . . Is that right?* The crowning jewel to letting the prospect know they're important is to show them how their input is used to get what they need.

In conclusion, put your ears to work and let your jaw muscles and vocal cords rest. And remember, the words *silent* and *listen* are made of the same letters.

~ 11 ~
Less is more

- Speak less, learn more.
- Focus on less, achieve more.
- Worry less, live more.

— 12 —

Silence is a necessity, not a negative.

– 13 –

Stop, ask, listen, and think before you respond

Stop!

Are you so caught up in the hairball of life that you rarely stop to reflect on where you are and what you need to change to improve your life?

Ask the right questions from the right people

These questions should be asked to your Personal Board of Directors. These are the three to five people you select who will tell you what you *need* to hear, not necessarily what you *want* to hear.

Listen to their answers

Don't bother asking the questions if you are not willing to listen objectively to their answers, as it would be a waste of time and energy. Capture their answers in writing—don't rely on your memory.

Think about the consequences

Remember that you, and only you, are responsible for your life choices and the consequences of such. By thinking about your choices before making decisions, you are more likely to respond (good!) than react (bad!). When you act before thinking *(ready, fire, aim!)*, you usually make poor decisions.

Respond appropriately

As you adhere to this four-step discipline, you will most often make good decisions that lead to a more fulfilling life. An illustration: When you have a follow-up visit to your physician after taking a prescribed medication for a sickness or illness, you receive one of the following diagnoses: "You are reacting (bad news)" or "You are responding (good news)." The previous four steps will help you to respond rather than react as you focus on making the right decisions for your life.

− 14 −
The likability factor

Why would anyone like you? Good question, isn't it? If you haven't answered it recently, do so. Then ask a couple friends or colleagues to provide answers to compare with yours.

You know the reason the answer to this question is so crucial: your prospects prefer buying from someone they like.

The difficulty with *likability* is that it's so subjective. What one person likes about you may not be what another person likes. So what do you do? Some people will simply tell you to "be yourself." Honestly, being yourself may not be good enough. Keep reading.

Your *friendliness* is a major ingredient in your likability factor. Before discussing the critical behaviors that will help you be more friendly, we should point out what you already know: that some salespeople have a more friendly personality than others. If you have a personality that is more introverted and find it difficult to engage prospects in a friendly conversation, you're going to have to practice improving your likability factor. Following are some tips on how to become more likable.

Smile

Your face is often the first part of you the prospect sees. Put a smile on it, because your prospects like to see a smiling face. Yes, certain personality types are more prone to putting smiles on their faces than others, so if you're one who finds it more of a challenge, put a smile on your face anyway. If need be, practice smiling while looking into a mirror until you can get a perfect smile ten times in a row. And complete these practice sessions until you are really, *really* good at smiling! ☺

Greet

You can also practice friendliness with every stranger you meet. Strangers don't know that you're practicing anything with them, so you don't have to worry about messing up. Share a friendly greeting and a warm smile with someone you don't know. Accept the challenge to offer a more sincere greeting than the Walmart greeter does to strangers. Think of the number of strangers whom you've thought about complimenting because they shared with you a sincere, warm smile and an enthusiastic, friendly greeting. Now you can be that stranger.

Focus on their interest

You're meeting with the prospect to talk to them. Instead of yielding to any temptation to talk about the exciting events or adversities occurring in your life, focus on the objective to talk about *them*. Listening is addressed in another article, so at the risk of being a bit redundant, keep in mind that you have two ears and one mouth—use them in proportion!

Care

Remember the cliché that no one cares what you know until they know how much you care. There are two critical components of caring. The first is caring about your prospect as an individual. You can do that by learning about the person's personal life, such as their family and hobbies. Be alert: some prospects are much more interested in the second caring component than the first, which is caring about their business and assisting them to be successful. You can read people. When it's obvious that the prospect's number one priority is business, talk business! You can learn more about the prospect as an individual as the relationship develops, but you won't get that chance if you don't start where they want to start. The important point is to show the prospect that he or she is the most important person in the world. Show that person that you are willing to do whatever you can to help them be successful. That's true caring in action.

~ 15 ~
The three things clients want

1. They want to trust you.
2. They want to like you.
3. They want you and your product or service to add value to their life.

– 16 –
The power of optimism

I want you to look at your left hand and find something about that hand you don't like. Perhaps it's the wrinkles or something about your fingernails. Now look for something you like about that hand, even if it's that you've got five working fingers. You just illustrated two very important principles. First, everything has both positive and negative characteristics. Second, how you see something is a matter of perspective. We always find what we look for, whether it's positive or negative. So what do you want to see, the positive or the negative characteristics of your selling situation? Best-selling author Wayne Dyer has stated, "When we change the way we look at things, things change the way they look." You'll decide what you see.

To be a successful salesperson, it is important to expect the best of every situation, to be an optimistic thinker. Being optimistic gives us hope, and hope is a tremendously important source of positive energy.

Authors Rick Hanson and Richard Mendius (*Buddha's Brain: The Practical Neuroscience of Happiness, Love, and Wisdom*) suggest that survival instincts hardwire humans to be pessimistic thinkers. That is, protecting ourselves from harm requires that we look at "what's wrong." Actually, research has concluded that we have about 50,000 independent thoughts per day, and 80 percent of these are negative in some fashion. Perhaps Hanson and Mendius are correct. One thing is for certain: you are not going to be a happy camper when you're thinking negative thoughts.

In reality, though, optimism is an internal natural resource, and you can have as much of it as you want by controlling your thoughts. The trick is to turn it on in an otherwise negative world. Just consider the wealth of negative information that bombards you every day, in addition to many prospects saying "no." Negative news is now available 24/7 through electronic media.

The psychological bottom line is that stemming the influence of genetics and the bombardment of negative information requires hard work. You must saturate your 50,000 daily thoughts with optimism. Fortunately, you can do that by putting the following formula to work.

1. Give one good reason to wake up

Each night before sleeping, think about one good reason you want to wake up in the morning. Consider the difference between the night before you go on vacation versus the night before you go to work. The night before vacation is flooded with positive energy and anticipation of the next day. You want every day to be like going on a vacation, so decide what you'll anticipate when you wake up every morning.

2. Oh, boy

Upon waking in the morning, tell yourself waking up is fantastic instead of hitting that snooze button. You want to begin the day with positive thoughts. Waking up is allowing you the opportunity to do what you want to do.

3. Visualize

While lying in bed for a few minutes, visualize being an optimistic person. See your day unfolding before you and you being optimistic and having fun.

4. Wake up early

Give yourself a mini-vacation on a daily basis. Wake up early enough to have time to do what you like to do. Doing so provides positive reinforcement for waking up each day.

5. Exercise

Awaken your body by completing simple stretching exercises. While conducting these exercises, think about the positive day you're preparing to experience. Good things are happening today!

6. Think: problems = opportunities

Notice the frequency at which you use the word *problem*. This word has a negative connotation, so even just thinking about it drains a bit of energy from your body. Remember Dyer's advice: "When you change the way you look at things, things change the way they look." Start replacing "problem" with "opportunity." *Opportunity* has a positive connotation, which gives you a positive boost of energy.

7. Act as if

There are two ways you can change your

behaviors. One is to change the way you think, and your behavior automatically changes. Sometimes, however, you must change your behavior first, such as by acting. After a while, your thinking changes to support the behavioral changes. Dale Carnegie stated, "Act enthusiastic, be enthusiastic." Acting enthusiastically is certainly an essential ingredient of optimism.

8. Look for the good

Remember looking for and finding something good about your hand? Develop the daily habit to look for the good, regardless of the negative situations you find yourself in. As you know, a prospect telling you "no" just means that you are one step closer to finding a prospect who will say "yes."

Use every day as a practice session. In other words, use the daily small frustrations to practice looking for the good. This will prepare you for when a truly negative experience knocks the wind from your sails.

$-17-$
SOW your way to sales success

Show up
On time
With a positive attitude.

— 18 —

Smile—customers like positive people.

– 19 –

Success is how high you bounce when you hit the bottom
—*General George Patton*

Selling is a tough job. You put yourself on the front line every day. After expending many hours working with the prospect and preparing the proposal, you optimistically expect a positive outcome only to hear the prospect say "no." That's the moment that two diametrically opposed energy sources (positive expectation of the sale, and a negative result— that nothing is going to happen) collide within your psyche. The result is frustration and disappointment. Sometimes the magnitude of these feelings can be overwhelming, and the disappointment knocks the wind from your sails. You may even be tempted to quit if the success ratio is not worth the pain.

Recalling that an eagle, despite its superior vision and speed, is successful at catching only about 10 percent of its prey offers little encouragement. It's easy to rationalize by saying with your superior intelligence, *You ought to be better than a stupid eagle.*

What do you do to bounce back?

You are human

You begin by accepting that you're human, and that feeling disappointed is therefore a natural reaction when your expectations get derailed. So be easy on yourself for feeling disappointed—that's a natural reaction.

You have options

Believe that you have options. You may not be able to control what happens to you, but you can control how you *respond* to what happens to you. One option is described in the words of Norman Vincent Peale, "We quit when we accept the image of defeat." Another option is to use the behavioral strategies listed below.

Use the magnetic pull

Perhaps the most important ingredient in being resilient is taking advantage of the magnetic pull emerging from where you want to go. That means keeping your eyes locked on where you want to go. A ski instructor once noted that people feeling out of control on a ski slope yield to the temptation to look at where they don't want to go. He advised to keep your eyes fixed on where you want your body to go. Instead of looking at the tree, look down the slope. He noted that your body follows your eyes. Keep your eyes locked on your goal, and continue to focus on the benefits associated with reaching your sales goals.

Be passionate

Dolly Parton is credited with stating, "When you love your work, you never have to go to work again." This can be true of your work in sales. The stronger your passion for your sales career, the more resistant you'll be to disappointment. A major element determining the intensity of your passion is your life's purpose. If you haven't defined your life's purpose yet, then do so. You want your career to be a natural extension of your purpose. My (Larry) purpose is to help people maximize their potential. That gives me the energy to awaken at 4 A.M. to write this book. It's not work—it's fun.

Give your sales career passion and fun by ensuring that it is a natural extension of your purpose to help people and organizations succeed. The more people you help to be successful, the more success you receive.

Be optimistic

Viktor Frankl survived the holocaust. As a psychiatrist and author (*Man's Search for Meaning*), he concluded that survivors were able to define a personal meaning for the traumatic experience. Frankl's advice would be to define what you learned when you were rejected by the prospect. Perhaps you've written the best proposal of your career but had it rejected. From that, you might learn more about what you can do to ensure that the next proposal is accepted. Or you could view the rejection as your practice and improvement at how to handle prospects who had the gall to tell you "no."

Frankl tells us to be optimistic and look for the good in things. Remember that you always find what you look for, and that optimism gives you hope. Hope is the energy that keeps us going during difficult times. When we lose hope, we accept the image of defeat, and that's not a good thing.

— 20 —

Each day you get better or worse.
It's your choice.

— 21 —

If you're selling on price alone,
you're an order taker, not
a professional.

— 22 —

We first make our habits and then our habits make us
—*John Dryden*

When a spiritual teacher and his disciples began their evening meditation, a cat that lived in the monastery made such a noise that it continually distracted them. One day the teacher ordered that the cat be tied up during the evening practice.

Years later, when the teacher died, the cat continued to be tied up during the meditation session. And when the cat eventually died, another cat was brought to the monastery and tied up. Centuries later, learned descendants of the spiritual teacher wrote scholarly treatises about the religious significance of tying up a cat for meditation practice.

The moral of this story for you is, What sales rituals do you engage in without questioning why? Are you stuck in your own personal rituals? Unfortunately, all of us can probably answer in the affirmative. The issue at hand is whether these rituals serve as best practices. If not, then you could be leaving sales on the table.

You're like an automobile—periodically, you need a tune-up. Sounds easy, but it may be more challenging than you think. You can look into a mirror to practice certain elements of your golf swing, but evaluating your sales rituals can be a very personal matter and thus not as easy to evaluate as your golf swing. First is the struggle to see the forest when you're among the trees. Second is that you may have been in sales for several years and are stuck in a rut and don't want to admit it. Third is the challenge to objectively evaluate the need for a tune-up. Fourth is the openness and willingness to accept the brutal truth about your performance. It's really all up to you and how good you really want to be.

World-class performers take advantage of a coach or teacher for one obvious reason—to close the gap between their "as is" situation and perfection. Hopefully, your sales manager can serve in this capacity. Having said that, let's also recognize that sometimes there are advantages to using a coach who's not your supervisor. Your supervisor may struggle to provide constructive feedback because of the potential to hurt your feelings. And, of course, you may have issues that you are just more comfortable discussing with an objective third party.

The working relationship with your coach is as crucial as the one between your prospect and you. You want to work with someone you trust and respect, who cares more about improving your performance than any fee that person may receive to assist you.

The bottom line is to obtain the assistance of someone (a colleague or professional sales coach) who can help evaluate your performance. Your objective is to make more effective habits so that these habits can help you be more effective.

− 23 −
20/80 principle

The 20/80 principle states that 20 percent of your activities produce 80 percent of your success. Now you need to figure out which 20 percent that is. The answer may be right in front of your nose.

If your company is like most, you have a defined system to secure leads, find qualified prospects, prepare proposals, keep in touch with prospects, and adhere to a sales strategy. Sales systems help you to be successful. The challenge is that you can easily be tempted to vary from this system. That can be a train wreck waiting to happen. History shows that daily routines completed on a consistent basis produce consistent positive results.

A friend of ours started his leadership development company by purchasing a franchise from a nationally recognized company. He, too, learned a sales system but elected not to follow it. After about six months, he became severely depressed because of his apparent business failure. After fighting his way through the depression, he decided to try the sales system he learned when he purchased the franchise. Magic began to happen. He subsequently won achievement awards for his consecutive years of being a peak producer.

We teach that *systems drive behavior changes.* You must define a personal system to develop the habit of using your company's systems. For example, schedule specific times within a day to complete the essential elements of your sales system. Then allow that schedule to control you.

To help you achieve this objective, spend time every morning thinking about having a great day using your company's sales system. Schedule a few minutes to read material that helps motivate you. The more you saturate your thinking with being successful through using the sales systems, the faster the behavior change. You will want to strategically place reminders and daily affirmations to help keep you on track during the course of the day.

Psychologists once taught that you could change a habit by consistently practicing a new behavior for twenty-one days. Current research in determining behavioral patterns shows that neural highways of specific neural synapses fire to guide behaviors. Changing behavior requires the creation of new neural highways, and that requires more than twenty-one days. The positive side is that the more you practice, the faster your behavior will change.

– 24 –

Identify and make a daily commitment to three "no-fail" activities.

— 25 —

Three steps to sales excellence and relationships that last

1. When customers understand you, you get their attention.
2. When customers trust you, you earn their loyalty.
3. When customers know that you really care, you catch their hearts.

– 26 –

If you burned bridges in the past, you better be able to walk on water in the future

Working with prospects is not always an enjoyable event. There are personality conflicts. There are prospects who continuously change their minds, want additional information, won't return telephone calls (after you jumped through hoops for them), and won't make a decision. The list goes on.

There are times when you would really like to tell a prospect how the cow eats the cabbage. Or at least let them know the frustrations they've put you through while trying to help them achieve higher degrees of success with your service or product. You would think they would be more appreciative. Unfortunately, some people just don't care.

Then, after some prospects become clients, you wish you could fire them. They transform into constant irritants and are high maintenance. And why is it that the smaller the account, the greater number of hassles that account generates?

Working with prospects and clients can be a pain! So what are you going to do about it? You've got several choices. First, you can refrain from expressing your frustration while continuing to jump through hoops. Second, you can vent your frustration in the privacy of your car or with your sales manager. Third, you can experience an emotional volcano and give them a piece of your mind.

If you're going to burn the bridge, you better be able to walk on water in the future. It's a small world, and you never know when you may need to walk across the burnt bridge. Plus, customer service research reports that a person has the tendency to share negative customer experiences with up to twenty-five people. Some of those twenty-five people may know you, or one may be a future prospect.

Rest assured, the prospect or client will most likely not own the frustrations they contributed to the workplace. It's not in your best interest to have the reputation of being difficult to work with.

You may not be able to control the irritants, but you can control your reaction to them. The best advice may be to flush the frustrations and move on. If you reach the boiling point, select the second option listed above, and go to the gym to rid yourself of the frustrations through a hard workout. Hopefully you've got a sales manager who is a good coach and can assist you in working through your emotional reactions. Words of caution, though: you may need to carefully consider the degree to which you discuss frustrations with your sales manager. You don't want to become an irritant to your sales manager, as you probably don't want him to do what you would like to do with the irritants in your life.

− 27 −

Today's struggles become the footsteps for tomorrow's successes

L ike you, we wish that success would be a straight-line function. But it's not. Actually, it's more like success equals 90 percent frustration and disappointment.

This formula may exist for legitimate reasons. First, bad things happen to good people. We're flooded with bad news 24/7. It's just part of Mother Nature. Second, survival of the fittest is very much alive in your workplace. Not every salesperson in your company or in your industry exhibits the degree of persistence that you do. Some of these salespeople will quit before reaching the blessing. Third, frustrations and disappointments provide an excellent classroom to learn the attitudes and skill sets to ensure your success. If selling were easy, everyone could do it, and then your career would be flooded with competition.

Another chapter in this book (Thing 27) focuses on resiliency, and you may want to re-read that chapter to help you deal with struggles that will arise. At the risk of being redundant, we want to emphasize the importance of *hope.* As long as we've got hope, *we won't quit before the blessing.* Hope stems from the continued excitement associated with achieving your sales goals. You want to escalate that excitement by flooding your thoughts with success and the benefits you and your family derive from a successful sales career. In fact, you want to put these benefits in writing, review them *every* morning, and strategically place the list to be seen and reviewed throughout the day.

To stimulate thought, we've started that list for you, and you can finish it.

Personal

1. Your sales career should emerge from your purpose in life. Thus, you are the right person in the right spot at the right time.
2. A sales career helps you maximize your potential. The first step to maximizing your potential is acquiring a positive attitude. You learn how to be optimistic by being adaptable and working through frustrations and disappointments. Second is continuously improving your sales skills.
3. You are in the process of using your career to make the best version of you.

Family

1. Your sales career may give you the flexibility to enjoy quality family time.
2. Your income stream provides opportunities for your family to enjoy life experiences that others do not.

Company

1. It feels great to be part of something greater than you and know that you're an integral component of your company's success.

You know that frustrations and disappointments are going to divert your focus from time to time. When that happens, exert the necessary control to refocus your eyes and keep them locked on your goals and the benefits of a successful sales career. Doing so puts fuel into your hope tank. Hope helps you use today's struggles as the footsteps leading to tomorrow's successes.

— 28 —

Be concerned when you lose, but never feel defeated.

— 29 —
Why are you afraid to risk?

Many sales professionals don't take risks because the best way to avoid failure is to avoid risk-taking. Instead, they choose the comfort zone and never experience the thrill of taking their sales career to the next level. The most successful sales professionals learn from their failures, adjust accordingly, and move on.

– 30 –
Why working harder doesn't always work

Success accelerates when you learn to slow down. You must learn to let go, relax, and refocus before you reengage another task. This is a way to prevent burnout. World-class sprinters understand the vital importance of rest between workouts and performances. As the Chinese proverb teaches us, "Muddy water, let stand, becomes clear." Get the right pace and grace in your day.

— 31 —

*Take time to recharge your
batteries. Rest is important.*

— 32 —
The rubber band syndrome

A Cat fell in love with a handsome young man and asked Venus to change her into the form of a woman so she would be attractive to the man. Venus consented to her request and transformed the Cat into a beautiful damsel. The young man was attracted to her, fell in love, and took her home as his bride.

While the man and bride were reclining in their chamber, Venus, wishing to discover whether the Cat in her change of shape had also altered her habits of life, let down a mouse in the middle of the room. The Cat, quite forgetting her present condition, started up from the couch and pursued the mouse, wishing to eat it. Venus was much disappointed and changed the Cat back to her former shape.

Imagine for just a moment using both of your hands to stretch a rubber band. The stretched rubber band has tension in its system, just as you experience tension when stretching yourself to change your behaviors to improve performance. What happens when you let loose the rubber band? Of course, it returns to its original state, thus removing the tension. Like the rubber band, you prefer to remain in a comfort zone, free from any tension. Consequently, unless you have a system to continue focusing on the behavior you are changing, like the Cat, you tend to return to your original behavior.

It matters not what behavior you're working to improve to become a better salesperson. Just remember the importance of putting a system to work for you. For example, if you are working to improve staying in touch with past clients, then enter that activity on your calendar instead of doing it when you find the time. As much as possible, reserve the same day of the week and hour for calling past clients, and this will become a natural part of your routine.

To ensure that you smile as you talk on the phone, use the old trick of putting a mirror on your desk, or put a smiley face on your phone. Your sales procedure may include a script to begin conversing with a prospect, and you may need to put that script by your phone as a reminder. The point is to define a system and hold yourself accountable to using the system.

Research concludes that world-class performers spend as many as 10,000 hours practicing. The focus of each practice session is to improve a very specific behavior, so these performers expect to be better subsequent to the intense practice session.

You should approach each day as a focused practice session instead of simply going through the motions. What do you want to improve today? At the end of the day, evaluate your performance. You can schedule focused role-playing sessions, but you're also practicing in real time with your prospects. Take advantage of every day and use the eight to ten hours as a focused practice session. If you adopt this discipline, you can be a world-class salesperson in about five years.

— 33 —
The PC formula for sales success

A re you ready to be challenged? Answer this question: What are the two critical ingredients for a successful sales career? Record your answers and keep reading.

Here's a true story illustrating that potential can be a curse. A sales manager explained that he's met many agents who he thought would be winners, but they failed because they lacked the passion and commitment to help people succeed in this profession. This manager explained that he continues to be as excited about his industry as when he started over thirty-three years ago. He explained that when, and if, he loses his passion, it's time to move on. Would you agree this is an excellent attitude for an individual seventy years young?

Consider another true story. The youngest sales agent (twenty-four years of age) in his organization is a top producer in his company. He credits his success to loving people and feels strongly that selling is a people-to-people business, not electronic transactions. He has a simple daily operating philosophy: *Life is good, people are good.*

The multiplier effect of *passion* and *compassion* produces tremendous energy to propel your success. You play with the numbers. Suppose you quantified the intensity of passion and compassion on a scale from one to ten. The ideal state is scoring a ten for each characteristic ($10 \times 10 = 100$). The higher your total score, the greater your likelihood of success.

We believe that both passion and compassion are natural resources waiting in your body to be developed. Unlike the physical natural resources that are being depleted by overuse, the more you use these psychological resources, the more you have to use.

Passion

Some authors believe that passion is a genetic gift. We're not supporters of that conclusion. Instead, we believe that passion emerges out of our life's purpose. Each of us has a reason to be here other than to consume natural resources. Unfortunately, most individuals have not devoted the time to finalize their personal purpose statement.

Begin thinking about answers to the following questions: Why are you here? What is your purpose in life? Clues to your answers may be included in what you really enjoy doing. Or think about the major experiences you've had, decisions you've made, or people in your life who have influenced you. How did each of these impact the adult reading this book?

Start putting your thoughts in writing, and eventually your purpose statement will emerge. As a salesperson, you've probably heard of the elevator story—being able to tell someone what you do during a sixty-second elevator ride. Use the same guideline as you finish writing your purpose.

Compassion

Compassion is caring for and enjoying helping others. Consider that people need to help each other to survive. As a salesperson, you are selling a service or product to help people become more successful in some manner. You exhibit compassion through showing your prospects how serious you are about wanting to improve their lives. It's more about them than about what you are selling. Your product or service is simply a tool to help people. In reality, you're in the business to help people. And helping through compassion speaks directly to the need for you to believe in the product or service you are selling.

To continue building your compassion, develop the habit of sharing your smile and a friendly greeting with the people you meet. Also, look for the opportunity to help those people. You'll find both of these habits to be enjoyable. That enjoyment will reinforce and thus encourage you to continue demonstrating compassion.

— 34 —

Sales success is high-touch, not high-tech.

– 35 –
The PNP formula

Selling is about building relationships. First, you sell you. Second, you sell your service or product. If you're not successful in selling you, chances are you won't have much of a chance to sell your service or product. The PNP formula is an excellent reminder of what you can do to sell you.

Plant the seeds of relationships.

Nourish them with random acts of recognition.

Pick the fruits of improved loyalty, relationships, and sales performance.

Plant seeds

Planting the seeds of relationships highlights the importance of you learning about the different social styles. To treat people like you would like to be treated is a great religious principle; it just doesn't work effectively in the business environment. Perhaps as many as 75 percent of your prospects don't want to be treated as you like to be. So start practicing the Platinum Rule, which is treating people the way they like to be treated.

Many models depicting working relationships use two psychological dimensions, assertiveness or willingness to be direct, and the degree that personal relationships are important. For example, some prospects, referred to as Drivers, want to focus on results while avoiding discussions on personal matters, while others—Amiables—enjoy talking about the personal matters before focusing on results. Another social style includes Analyticals, who prefer to talk about logic, numbers, and procedures. Then there is the one known as Expressives, who adhere to the "variety is the spice of life" principle. You can talk about anything with an Expressive.

You need to be able to identify your prospect's style to be able to connect with them quickly and be liked.

Nourish seeds

Now that you've connected, you want to nourish the relationship. Random acts of "thinking of you" is an especially effective fertilizer. That is, periodically send articles, birthday cards, and related messages to show the prospect that you're thinking about them. Such periodic messages also help keep them aware of your presence among all the noise generated by other salespeople.

Pick the fruit

Picking ripe fruit—or enjoying an effective relationship—depends upon how you treat the prospect. Drivers are most interested in establishing relationships with people who are businesslike and focus on achieving results. Expressives connect with people who display energy, a sense of humor, and a willingness to discuss a variety of subjects. Amiables want to know that you care about them as individuals. Analyticals focus on the thoroughness of how you present information.

As a sales professional, you are a student of behavior. We recommend that you read *The Platinum Rule: Discover the Four Basic Business Personalities—and How They Can Lead You to Success* by Tony Alessandra and Michael O'Connor to learn more about connecting with different people.

— 36 —
Selling differently to different people

We introduced you to the concept of working differently with different people in the preceding chapter. The focus of this chapter is to extend that concept to selling differently to different people. Obviously, space limits the degree of detail that can be provided in this chapter. Thus, to learn more about this principle, we encourage you to read *Relationship Selling: The Eight Competencies of Top Sales Producers* by Jim Cathcart. Now let's focus on the highlights.

Drivers

Drivers need to know the expected results to achieve by using your product or service. What is the return on the financial investment? When selling to a

Driver, be confident, concise, to the point, and businesslike. Refrain from small talk unless the Driver initiates it. When the selling episode is finished, remain only if the Driver encourages you to. Be cautious to not overstay your welcome.

Expressives

The Expressive is a bundle of energy who is interested in talking about anything and everything, particularly if he can use the *I* pronoun. It's important to connect with the Expressive by matching his energy and enthusiasm. The selling process needs to focus on "sound bites" of information. Show how the sound bites emerge from something the Expressive has said. You can even take advantage of his competitive spirit—e.g., *Can you imagine the competitive advantage you'll have by . . . ?* You may struggle to keep the Expressive on target, but an easy way to do that is by asking questions to direct them back to the subject matter.

It is important to structure the immediate next steps. If you leave it to the whim of the Expressive, there may not be any next steps. Another important characteristic to remember is that the Expressive wakes up in a new world every day. Thus, strike while the fire is hot. Structure the deal and put it in writing as quickly as you can.

Amiables

The Amiable prefers close relationships. She wants to know that you care about her as an individual. So the initial conversation needs to focus on the Amiable as an individual. Dale Carnegie teaches that everyone has a family, hobby, and pets—these can serve as conversation starters. Talking about the Amiable's personal and professional story is very important.

Be prepared for a sales process that will require time. The Amiable wants to be certain you are trustworthy and care about her success; in other words, you are selling you. The Amiable wants to know why she should want to buy from you. Once that is determined, you can proceed to sell your product or service.

Analyticals

Get ready to provide reams of detail. The Analytical is a calculated, detailed problem solver. He likes documentation and data showing the results achieved through your product or service. Any data comparing the benefits of what you're selling to what your competitors are selling can also be helpful. Be certain to ask what additional information is needed to help the Analytical make a decision. Be sure that submitted information is correct, accurate, and delivered before you promise it. Focus on exceeding his expectations when you provide requested information.

As you learn to sell to the different social styles, you will increase your closing ratio.

~ 37 ~
Confusing activity with getting results

A gentleman named John Henry Faber conducted an experiment with processionary caterpillars, which derive their name from their peculiar habit of blindly following each other wherever they are going and in the specific order they are lined up. Faber placed the caterpillars in a circle and for twenty-four hours, the caterpillars dutifully followed one another around and around. Then Faber placed the caterpillars on a round saucer full of pine needles (their favorite food). For six days, the mindless creatures moved around and around the saucer, literally dying of starvation and exhaustion even though an abundance of choice food was located less than two inches away. You see, they had confused activity with accomplishment.

It's easy to get into the activity trap as a salesperson and spend an inordinate amount of time being busy by organizing files, materials, your desk . . . the list goes on. It's great to be organized, but not at the expense of your high payoff activities, such as maintaining your contact list, calling prospects, filling your sales' pipeline, keeping in contact with both prospects and clients, and attending networking functions. You may need to put activities into two categories: (1) high payoff leading to sales, and (2) staying busy. You need a personal system that helps you control your time to ensure that you spend 80 percent of your time completing those tasks that lead to sales.

– 38 –
Choose effectiveness over efficiency.

– 39 –

You receive what you share with others

What is the number one reason you are in sales? Give it some thought before spontaneously spouting off an answer, as your answer will have a major impact upon your success.

1. To make money. Are you sure? Money is important, as you need it to cover basic needs. Money also allows you to fulfill ego needs, such as a nice house, the right schools for your children, and nice cars.

Here's the red flag. You don't want your prospect to know that making money is your major driver. Now here's the kicker. You may think that you're successfully hiding the intensity of your drive to make money. Research is now concluding that you send messages to your prospect that she unconsciously receives. Your prospect then unconsciously uses that information to prepare her response. Scary, isn't it?

What is the likely outcome if your prospect believes that you are trying to sell her your product or service simply to advance your personal agenda? Automatically, the prospect will resist your efforts. If you don't care about her, then why should she care about you? If you're only after money, you may be shooting yourself in the foot before your big race. Obviously, you don't want to do that if you want to win the race.

2. To serve. This is a better answer. First and foremost, your career is to help your prospects be successful. You want to send the message both consciously and unconsciously that you care about serving your prospect's needs. You do that by using the advice offered in this book to build relationships, listening to understand the prospect's needs, and showing him how your product or service fits his needs. You want the prospect to feel as though he is your most important relationship.

There is an ironic outcome—when you stop chasing money and start serving others, money often finds you. The more you serve, the more you succeed.

Paradigm shift

If by chance your answer was money, or if you disagree with our position in this chapter, then it may be time for you to give the purpose of your sales career very serious consideration. The odds are that you're not going to get very far with a self-serving attitude. Should you question our position, you only have to look at self-serving attitudes expressed within your company to learn the error of these ways. Another resource is the best-selling book *Egonomics: What Makes Ego Our Greatest Asset (Or Most Expensive Liability)* by David Marcum and Steven Smith. These authors point out that self-serving behaviors cost organizations up to 21 percent of their operating budget. That's not a pretty picture. Another factor to consider is the degree to which you need people just to survive—that is, other people make your clothes, cars, food, et cetera. We're sure you get the picture.

You may be wondering how to shift your focus to service. Begin by rendering services to those around you. Volunteer to assist family and coworkers whenever possible. Provide as much service as you can to your prospects. Express friendliness to strangers. Review a couple chapters of this book daily to serve as a continuing reminder to serve prospects. The more you serve, the more success you will achieve.

– 40 –
There is no = in relationships

There are no "equal signs" in true client relationships. The most successful sales professionals do the little things (such as sending handwritten notes and small gifts) without expecting anything in return.

Ironically, those who practice this philosophy ultimately receive much more than they give. This is a way of expressing how much you truly care and value your client relationships, and it will separate you from the crowd of order takers.

When you focus on giving without expecting anything in return, your sales career will magically flourish. Try it!

— 41 —

Are you good enough to get better?

Y ou've got to be competent to realize your in-competence. The more competent people know, the more they realize they don't know. Competent people are continuously striving to improve their competence. They realize that when they stop trying to improve, they're through.

The following figure examines the relationship between being aware and levels of competence.

	Competent	**Not Competent**
Aware	Good	Good
Not Aware	Good	Not Good

As you can see, awareness is a key factor. It is imperative for you to know who you are in order to maximize your strengths and continuously improve your areas of weakness. There should be no need to dwell on this point. Sometimes, however, you may not be aware of your strengths as seen through the eyes of others. We suspect that this is a common occurrence.

The danger point is not being aware of your levels of incompetence—when other people recognize your incompetence but you don't. Such blind spots can derail your career. For example, a salesperson—we'll call him Mark—was a bundle of energy and could engage lively conversation on just about any subject. The problem is he continuously "talked over" people to the point that coworkers and clients complained about his behavior. When confronted with this reality, Mark was shocked and denied it. Mark's position was that he was just being friendly. Mark could not see himself as others saw him.

You want to be a student of yourself. To do so requires you to become a professional at being aware and into the moment. The pleasure-pain principle is a major contributor to your willingness to learn about you. Learning about your strengths can be fun, but learning about your weaknesses can be painful, thus the initial temptation to avoid such discomforting information. The key that opens the door to accepting this discomfort is being okay with whatever you learn. Not only do you need to accept that you'll be "okay" (the discomfort won't be so painful that you cannot cope with it), you must also recognize the benefits from receiving this information. Recognizing the benefits can likewise help you overcome the temptation to avoid learning the ugly truths.

Some people believe that self-awareness is a genetic gift—you either have the gift or you don't. We're more optimistic and believe that you can learn to be more self-aware. Mother Nature has provided you access to the self-knowledge that we're addressing in this chapter. For example, you can examine your thoughts, feelings, and behaviors. You can also complete self-assessments that provide information about your strengths and weaknesses in specific psychological characteristics and skill sets. Your human resources department can serve as a resource for you. The last window to look through to learn about you is obtaining feedback from others.

A starting point in becoming more self-aware is to write your life's story. Doing so means identifying your most significant negative and positive (1) experiences, (2) critical decisions made, and (3) people who served as role models. Record how each of these impacted your development.

Throughout the day, practice being self-aware or into the moment. Spend a couple of minutes examining your current thoughts and feelings. After significant interactions with others, examine how your actions impact them.

Another valuable exercise is to conduct several brainstorming sessions to list what you consider your strengths and weaknesses. As you complete this exercise, be acutely aware of the emotional temptation to not list a certain characteristic. List it anyway and asterisk it. Later, think about those that you've asterisked, as those strengths and weaknesses may describe you more than you like to think.

You can take this exercise to another level by asking your supervisor, coworkers, or friends to list your strengths and weaknesses. Doing so requires you to use the *gift of feedback,* which is the subject of the next chapter.

Improving your self-awareness requires a time commitment and hard work on your part, but you will find this historical journey to be richly rewarding.

– 42 –
The gift of feedback.

Receiving constructive feedback is certainly a gift. Your position within your company provides ample opportunities to receive feedback from your prospects and clients as well as from your supervisor. Are you ready to receive the feedback that is critical to your personal development as a salesperson?

Before answering that question, consider the special role feedback plays in your life. Your nervous system is designed to obtain the critical feedback to help you get through the day. You couldn't even pick up a pen or a cup of coffee without Mother Nature's gift of feedback. Another example of the importance of feedback is having a map or GPS when traveling to an unknown destination; without this feedback, we would get lost. (Have we made the point about the importance of feedback?)

Selecting an option

Here's your challenge. You get defensive when receiving feedback that is not complimentary, even if you know it is true. Your defensiveness is based on the survival instinct, as your body is trying to protect you from harm. So, one option is that you can yield to the temptation and deny the feedback. Seeing no evil, hearing no evil, speaking no evil can be an effective defense mechanism, but it can derail your sales career as well. Or you may even accept the feedback as the truth, but for whatever reason decide not to act on it. Perhaps too much work is required to change. Or admitting the weakness is a serious blow to your ego.

To receive the *gift of feedback,* you must override your natural tendency to avoid it. Competent salespeople recognize feedback plays a special role to help them (1) identify gaps between the "as is" situation and where they want to go, and (2) provide critical information as they strive to improve performance. Without feedback, they're lost, and being lost is not going to get them to where they want to go!

Comfortable in your skin

To be open to receive the *gift of feedback,* it's important to be confident and comfortable with yourself. You acquire confidence as you learn and grow. Confidence is one of those unlimited natural resources—the more you use, the more you get. This speaks to the very heart of being the professional who is continuously stepping out of your comfort zone to grow.

If you should not have the confidence level to be comfortable receiving feedback, then you *must act as if.* What that means for you is you must literally act as though you are comfortable in your skin. At those moments when you don't feel that way, you exert the necessary self-control to tell yourself to relax and be in control. Your body will be inclined to become tense, so you should adopt a more comfortable physical position.

Begin looking for the good in this particular situation immediately. You'll find what you're looking for, and as you find the positive characteristics of the feedback session, you'll begin to relax.

Now for perhaps the most important bit of advice: the more frequently you put yourself into the position to receive and use constructive feedback, the more confident you become at being in this position. So put yourself into the position to seek and use feedback as frequently as you can. This confidence will help you be comfortable within your own skin.

Competence requires hard work, but hard work paves the road to success.

– 43 –

Ask your customers to audit your performance. Their opinion is the only one that counts.

Wisdom of the oak

The oak tree is a great metaphor for life. Like our lives, the oak requires moisture to grow. The moisture of life is the truth. As long as we are vulnerable and open to absorbing the truth, we remain vibrant and are able to withstand the inevitable storms of life, including the downs of the sales profession. Once we cut ourselves off to truth, we become hardened and brittle. Like the oak without water, the challenges of life will slowly but surely break us apart, leaving us a shell of what we could have become if we had only been open to absorbing the truth.

Is your life and sales career moist and growing or dry and rotting? The good news is that it's never too late to start creating the sales legacy you want to leave behind.

Following are a few recommendations on how you can benefit from the awesome power of truth:

Seek It – Speak It – Expect It – Respect It – Live It

— 45 —
It's not about you

Top sales professionals are like the majestic oak tree: they spend their careers growing and giving back.

– 46 –
The power of self-talk

Research has concluded that you have 50,000 independent thoughts per day. In reality, you are constantly talking to yourself, so it's easy to forget the power harnessed in this thinking. Your thinking determines how you feel. Start thinking about a tragic event in your life and immediately, you start feeling sad or experience other downbeat feelings. Conversely, start thinking about an enjoyable activity, and your feelings become more upbeat. You have control of your feelings simply by controlling your thoughts. That's the challenge.

Write down the first thought that appears in your conscious mind when you read the following statement: *You can make $250,000 per year.* We're guessing your answer falls into one of these three categories: (1) No, (2) I don't know (doubt), or

(3) Yes, I can. We encourage you not to spend the money on this book if your answer falls into the first two categories.

Research has also concluded that the average person has 40,000 negative thoughts a day (these are placed in the first two categories in the previous paragraph). That's a whopping 80 percent of your 50,000 daily thoughts. It seems that your thinking is both your worst enemy as well as your best friend. This struggle between positive and negative thinking is going on inside your mind every day.

Rick Hanson and Richard Mendius explain the preponderance of negative thinking in their book *Buddha's Brain: The Practical Neuroscience of Happiness, Love, and Wisdom.*

1. Negative thinking and anxiety have had the most impact upon survival.
2. The brain detects negative information faster than positive.
3. Negative experiences are stored in the hippo-

campus for immediate future reference.

4. Negative events have more of an impact than positive ones. That is, people work harder to avoid a loss than to acquire a gain. It generally takes five positive interactions to counter the effects of just one negative interaction.

5. Negative experience leads to a vicious cycle, making you pessimistic and negative on yourself.

You're not going to be a successful salesperson while thinking ugly thoughts. You want to strive to make 80 percent of your thoughts positive ones, but to do that you must override the built-in negative biases. Doing so requires hard work.

While you're reading this book, pick up an ink pen. Find something about the pen that you don't like or would change. Now find something about the pen you like. While you're thinking about and looking for the negative, you won't see the positive, and vice versa. Take advantage of that mutually exclusive thinking to train yourself to look for the good in every situation. That's hard to do in a world dominated by bad things happening to good people. Combine that negative reality with the fact that only 10 to 20 percent of your qualified prospects will buy from you.

The psychological bottom line is that you have a choice: think negatively or positively. You want to start with the end in mind. Schedule time every morning to fill your psychological tank, and begin the day with positive expectations. Every morning re-read this article or others that we've included on being positive and resilient to serve as a reminder of the person you are going to be today.

There will be times during the course of the day when you must force yourself to think positively in spite of the negativity that surrounds you. Listing the benefits of those situations that tempt you to be negative is a good way to force yourself to think positively. There is a lot of power in positive thinking, and we hope you take advantage of that power.

— 47 —
10,000 hours

Have you wondered what the difference is between a world-class athlete and one who is good but not world-class? Does one have more talent than the other?

There is an ongoing debate about the origin of talent. Is talent genetically determined, or do you learn it? This question is most frequently asked in reference to athletes, musicians, and other high-profile individuals. However, the same question applies to the sales profession. Obviously, some salespeople are more successful than others. Do genetics contribute to these differences, or is it a matter of luck?

In his best-selling book *Talent is Overrated: What Really Separates World-Class Performers from Everybody Else,* Geoff Colvin advances the position that hard work is the primary ingredient determining world-class performance. More specifically, the differentiating feature is that such performers spend at least 10,000 hours in focused practice. Focused practice means that each practice session is designed to improve a specific aspect of their performance. These individuals expect their performance to improve as the result of this focused practice.

The willingness to spend 10,000 focused practice hours speaks to the issue of intrinsic versus extrinsic motivational factors. Intrinsic include those motivational forces that are within you—e.g., enjoyment, a sense of purpose, and accomplishment. Extrinsic factors include things you receive, like sales contest prizes and awards. Of the two factors, intrinsic is the more powerful and lasting motivational source.

World-class performers are driven to do whatever is required to be the best they can be. Yes, they want to win, but they enjoy the pursuit of perfection—they are intrinsically motivated.

Now back to you. How much time do you spend in focused practice? Your answer will provide insight into the degree to which you are driven to be the best salesperson you can be. Using the 10,000-hour formula, you can be a world-class salesperson within five years if you use each day as a focused practice session. At the beginning of every day, you should decide the specific sales behavior that you want to practice. How are you going to be different at the end of the day compared to the beginning of the day?

～ 48 ～

Work harder and smarter.

– 49 –
The power of enthusiasm

Everyone agrees that enthusiasm is an important behavioral ingredient to improve both the quality of your life and your career, because it helps you feel positive and energetic. Plus, it's contagious. What is its origin? Is it genetically determined, or do you acquire it? When considering a human's first experience in this world, one has to wonder how anyone can learn to be enthusiastic. Most people spend nine blissful months within their mother. Then one day, the birthing process occurs. You leave a quiet environment and enter a noisy one. Mom's womb was dark, and now the bright lights hurt your eyes. You have now emerged from a quiet, peaceful world into one that's full of noise and hustle and bustle. And then the doctor slaps your behind. Supposedly, that slap is to assist your breathing, but psychologically, the slap told you that the honeymoon is over—this is a tough world out here! How do you become enthusiastic after experiencing such traumatic imprinting experiences?

To complicate the matter, *enthusiasm* is a rather abstract word. What behaviors constitute enthusiasm? The Greek root of the word is *entheos,* meaning "God from within." How do you teach someone or learn how to act like *God from within?* We believe that you can learn to be more enthusiastic and offer you the following behavioral definitions.

"I can" thinking

Positive expectations are touchstones for enthusiasm. You have a choice to think either negatively ("I can't," or expressing doubt) or positively (asserting "you can"). Enthusiastic salespeople gush forth with excited "I can" thinking.

Optimism

Enthusiastic salespeople have trained themselves to look for the good in spite of the flood of negative news and experiences. They understand that every experience has both positive and negative characteristics, and they choose to focus on the positive ones.

Results-oriented

Enthusiastic salespeople live purpose-driven lives—they've defined and are living their purpose. The results they desire to achieve in life are a direct extension of their life's purpose. That combination produces passion, which is the fuel for high performance.

People power

Enthusiastic salespeople realize the importance of acting in ways to encourage others to both like and want to work with them. Doing so creates synergy through cooperation. They understand the formula $1 + 1 = 3$—that is, a third mind is created whenever two people work together, helping them to generate ideas that neither would have thought of on their own. Enthusiastic salespeople understand that they receive what they share with others. Thus, they focus on helping others to be successful.

Self-confidence

Enthusiastic salespeople face their fears and step out of their comfort zones. They understand that such risks are crucial to learning self-confidence and maximizing their potential to be the very best version of themselves. Such people adhere to the principle discussed by Catherine Ponder: "Failure is success trying to be born in another way."

Self-esteem

Last, but certainly not least, is liking yourself. Doing so is such an important source of emotional energy. Enthusiastic salespeople understand their self-esteem is a matter of choice. They adhere to the principle that what happens to you is important, but your reaction to what happens to you is even more important. They understand that self-esteem is a choice. Instead of believing messages they've received that they are "not good enough," they elect to believe they are good people and like themselves anyway. As you know, self-esteem is a very powerful emotional energy source, and enthusiastic people want to use it to promote their quality of life and sales careers.

Sales is a challenging career, so you want to use every tool that's available to make it simpler and more worthwhile. Enthusiasm is one of those important tools to have in your tool kit.

– 50 –
Choosing to succeed

Success is a decision according to David Byrd, author of *Achievement: A Proven System for Next-Level Growth.* According to Byrd, you must make a choice about your attitude, action, and accountability.

Attitude

Your body is designed to be in a state of balance or status quo. Immediately, you see the problem with this. Remaining in the status quo probably won't get you where you want to go. We've spoken about the average person thinking 40,000 negative thoughts a day. Thinking is an inherent component to being a human being, and negative thinking may have been developed to protect us. Consequently, negative thinking may be instinctive. You're not going to eliminate negative thinking, so that puts you in the position to make a very important decision. Are you going to decide to let negative thinking keep you safe and comfortable in your comfort zone? Or are you going to make the decision to take control of your thoughts and engage in thinking that will lead you to success?

The largest word contained in the word *impossible* is *possible.* It is imperative for you to believe that it's possible for you to take your sales career to the next level. To do so, your thoughts must lead the way. You'll initially reach the next level with your thoughts, and your actions will follow. Begin thinking that you've already achieved your goal. Think and act like you already possess the qualities of being at the next level in your sales career.

Actions

Effective actions deliver desirable results. Again, it's *your choice* how you spend your time. Do you spend 80 percent of your time engaging in actions that lead you to the next level of your sales career? Or do you fill your days with activities that are leading you nowhere?

There is a very simple process to ensure that your daily actions deliver results. First, establish your yearly goals and then your monthly goals. Second, decide which key performance indicators must be reached at a monthly, weekly, and daily basis to achieve your goals. Third, decide what you must do every day in order to achieve your goals. How many prospects and existing customers must you talk to on a daily basis? What articles or notes must you send to keep in touch with your contacts? What networking activities will you participate in on a regular basis?

Personal accountability

Accountability is nothing more than doing what you need to do at the time you need to do it. Exhibiting personal accountability is really an exercise in self-discipline. The most effective system to ensure self-discipline is to schedule the completion of every activity. Then, let your calendar take control of your life.

– 51 –

If you're not keeping score, you're just practicing.

$-52-$
The Law of Expectation

R honda Byrne's best-selling book *The Secret* speaks to this powerful law. When published, the book was immediately surrounded by a storm of controversy, which stemmed from the author's position that all one has to do is think about something happening and it will happen. The point made by the detractors is the expectation that you can literally get whatever you want by simply thinking about it—the old "get-something-for-nothing" principle—is a false assumption.

How do you prefer to start your day? Expecting that you are going to close a sale today, or expecting that all of your prospects are going to say no? We think the answer is obvious. In expecting success, you're using the Law of Expectation as your friend. Starting the day expecting failure would be a doomsday. That's using the Law of Expectation as an enemy, which doesn't sound like a lot of fun.

The Law of Expectation, or expecting positive results, is powerful. First, it sets your attitude or your psychological environment. Second, expecting a positive result not only helps you to feel better and more energetic to focus on your high-payoff activities, but it is likewise contagious. Your coworkers and prospects can see and feel your positive attitude and consequently will enjoy being around you. For just a moment, imagine your prospect's response to your attitude of expecting him not to buy from you. Your prospect would probably prefer not being around you. Third, the Law of Expectation underwrites the assumptive closing technique—you just act as if you assume your prospect is going to buy. You probably recognize the pressure that technique would put on your prospect.

The Law of Expectation has been misinterpreted. It is not a law for the lazy salesperson. The Law of

Expectation sets the stage; you must still get onto the stage and do the acting. You've got to be a person of action to get results. As you strive to reach the goals included within your Law of Expectation, opportunities present themselves, and you'll notice additional ones. Are these opportunities coincidental? We don't believe in coincidences; things happen for a reason, and there is an order in this universe. Working in accordance with the Law of Expectation can transform your life.

With all that said, best-selling author Wayne Dyer believes in manifestation. He argues that as you think about what you want to happen in your life, you actually bring that event closer to you. Both of us are living examples that the Law of Expectation works. We have written several books and live with the expectation that we'll write additional ones. This book is the result of Byrd responding to an e-mail from Turner Publishing. Is the fact that Byrd received the initial e-mail a coincidence?

Both of us have as many questions about all the forces within this universe as you do, but we know that right now you can put the Law of Expectation to work for you and your sales career. To do so, you need a crystal-clear image of what you want to achieve, expect to reach the goal, and start taking the necessary actions to make your goal a reality. As you do, opportunities will knock. You just need to open the door and let opportunity enter.

— 53 —

Is your sales career a self-fulfilling prophecy?

Do you believe that you have or can have a successful sales career? Do you think about developing your potential to be better than you are today? Or do you worry about not having the necessary skill sets or self-confidence to be successful? Do you have a crystal-clear image of success? What do your private daydreams tell about you? Do these daydreams focus on positive or negative consequences in your life? You may be one of the fortunate ones who answers these questions positively. Others, unfortunately, don't.

Consider for a moment the impact of your thinking upon your career. Is your thinking a self-fulfilling prophecy? Earl Nightingale stated, "We become what we think about." In other words, can you fly with the eagles when you think you're a chicken? Nightingale thinks you'll act like a chicken.

Researchers have done an experiment on behavior modification by placing fleas in a cup with a lid. After the fleas jumped and repeatedly hit their heads against the lid for a period of time, the researchers removed the lid, and the fleas no longer attempted to jump out. The fleas learned that they could not win and modified their behavior. What modifications have you made to your sales performance based on your beliefs? Strange as it may seem, there are those who believe they do not deserve success. When faced with the possibility of achieving more success than that person believes he deserves, he modifies his behavior to sabotage it. We hope this description does not fit you.

Beliefs have powerful control over your life. Your beliefs guide your behavior, and your behavior determines your level of success. You want to be the person who believes you are a winner and deserves to win, taking advantage of Nightingale's sage advice. To take control of your thought pattern is a difficult but achievable assignment. First, you must believe that you are capable of controlling your thoughts in spite of their spontaneous, uncontrollable nature. Do you see the self-fulfilling prophecy at work in this statement? Second, when spontaneous thoughts occur that interfere with your image of success, you must tell yourself to stop. Ask yourself if you want to make a good or bad choice. The good choice is obviously changing your thought pattern to focus on your winning image. Third, you want to act as if you are guaranteed success. We don't want you to be arrogant but rather to act confidently.

Hard work is required to significantly change your habitual thought pattern (re-read the chapter on 10,000 hours), but you have much to gain since your life is a self-fulfilling prophecy. What do you want your prophecy to say about you?

– 54 –
Getting in sync with Mother Nature

We've discussed the power of thinking and your tendency to be hardwired to think negative thoughts. Here's the contradiction that requires consideration.

A major differentiator between humans and other living plants and animals is our ability to think and reason, i.e., the ability to apply logic. For a moment, think about the focus of all "nonthinking" plants and animals—being all they can be based on the resources available for growth. In other words, they are spontaneously growing and developing to be the best version of themselves. A tree growing out of rocks doesn't reach the majestic heights of one that is growing in fertile soil. But what is it doing? It's being everything that it can be according to the available resources. It's not complaining about growing out of the rocks versus the more fertile soil. It's just growing.

Now back to humans. We have the most powerful information processor known to mankind located right between our ears. Yet we've discussed that 80 percent of our thoughts are negative in some fashion, and such thoughts sabotage success.

The contradiction is, like the nonthinking plants and animals, you are equipped with the tool to maximize yourself. We believe that being the best you is a universal purpose of life—it's the natural thing to do. So on the one hand, you may be hardwired to be negative, but on the other hand, Mother Nature's way is for you to utilize the resources available to you to be the best you. But to do that you've got to exert the necessary self-discipline to utilize the resources, which includes your thought pattern. In other words, you've got to override the natural tendency to be negative. You would think that since maximizing you is Mother Nature's way, combined with all the enjoyment of maximizing your potential to improve the quality of your life and advance your career, that thinking positively would be easier than it is.

Isn't it interesting how so many things you need to do to be successful revert to being self-disciplined?

In some ways, it seems life would be easier if we were all like trees. They don't think about using resources, they simply do what comes naturally.

Self-discipline is a key to success

The strength of your will is critical to your success. You know your company's sales process yields success. The challenge is consistently doing what you know is right. The discipline required to meet your own expectations requires hard work. You would be so much stronger if there weren't so many temptations that seem a lot more fun than the work required to be successful.

So how do you strengthen your willpower?

1. Focus on the disadvantages

What happens if you don't adhere to your company's sales process? That price may include such things as not making the sales necessary to maintain your family's lifestyle, or letting both your team and company down. You may even experience guilt. Generate your list. The negative consequences should be ugly enough that you automatically make the decision, "Falling off the wagon and not doing what is right is not an option." You want to be pushed toward doing what is right.

2. Focus on your benefits

Build an epidemic of excitement to keep you focused on doing what needs to be done. List the advantages you'll accrue as the result of successfully following your company's sales process. Those advantages will surely include such things as working to maximize your potential; helping your customers, team, and company to achieve higher levels of success; and providing the essential income for your family. Take the time to generate your own list of benefits.

Your challenge is doing what must be done to keep these at the forefront of your mind, otherwise referred to as top-of-mind awareness. For example, review these in the morning; you may post them in your office or car as continuous reminders throughout the day. You want the excitement to build to the point that it literally pulls you through completing the sales process. You want to feel as though it is ridiculous to have even been tempted to do something else. But you're human, and you'll be tempted. Then what do you do?

3. Stop and think

The essence of self-control is exercised when you're tempted to vary from what you know needs to be done. You must take control of your decision-making process to do what is right. At that critical point, tell yourself to stop and think. Ask, "Do I want to make a good choice or a bad one?" Psychologically, the pleasure of the good choice over the frustration associated with a bad choice should be enough to tip the energy scales to make a good choice. Sometimes the temptation may be stronger, and that requires extra effort on your part. Before you decide, think about the disadvantages of yielding to temptation along with the benefits of making the right choice.

You're human, so even with these tools at your disposal, there are going to be times when you yield to temptation and fail to complete the essential sales process. When that happens, experience the disappointment and use it to get you back on track. What did you learn from getting off track? Learn something that will benefit you and make it easier to stay focused the next time temptation raises its ugly head.

We, like you, wish life could be easier. But a lot of self-discipline is required to be a successful salesperson.

— 56 —
Time: manage it well

Native American wisdom teaches us that there are three things that don't come back: an arrow spent, words spoken, and time passed. Use every minute like it may be your last, and learn like you will live forever.

~ 57 ~
It's not the big things that hold us back

Our sales career will grow to the next level when we learn to do the small things on a consistent basis. David Noonan says, "In the end, it is attention to detail that makes all the difference. It's the center fielder's extra two steps to the left, the salesman's memory for names, the lover's phone call, the soldier's clean weapon. It is the thing that separates the winners from the losers, the men from the boys, and, very often, the living from the dead."

– 58 –

It's not the big things that you do for your clients that make you successful. It's the small things done on a consistent basis.

~ 59 ~
You must change as the world changes

A company—we'll be creative and call it Don't Know Our Customers—has enjoyed the reputation of being the leader in their marketplace. The sales department has had the luxury, or perhaps enjoyed a bit of arrogance, of consistently receiving requests for proposals. Do you get the picture that they sat in their nice offices waiting for the next opportunity to come knocking at their door?

In today's market, the company is experiencing competitors who are buying business. Consequently, Don't Know Our Customers is experiencing a new phenomenon—although they still have the best product in the marketplace and a reputation of providing excellent customer service, the competition is eating their lunch.

A new sales manager entered the picture and was appalled to learn that salespeople, being creatures of habit, did not attempt to meet prospects before submitting their final sales proposals. I'm sure you can imagine the sales staff's response when the sales manager suggested the importance of developing relationships. The choir sang the song, *"That's not the way we do business around here!"* Evidently, the salespeople were not aware of how the definition of insanity—continuing to do what you've always done and expecting a different result—applied to them! We hope you agree there is no future in being insane.

Now is the time to use every arrow in your quiver to change as the world changes. It is time to remind yourself that organizations change when people change. The Don't Know Our Customers company needs to change. The moral of that story for you is that an ever-changing marketplace may cause your company to sell differently than it has in the past. Having the reputation of being stuck in the past may not be conducive to a healthy sales career. You want the reputation of being a creative change agent who develops and implements the necessary strategies essential to leading your company into tomorrow.

— 60 —

If you're not changing, you're not in first place.

– 61 –

You are literally unable to to perceive data right before your eyes

Oops, you may have missed something—re-read the title of this chapter again. Did you notice that the word *to* is repeated?

It's interesting how we get locked in and fail to see reality right before our eyes. We see what we expect to see rather than reality.

Your imagination will play tricks on you. What do you begin assuming when a prospect doesn't return your call? That they're not interested, right? How many times have you later learned that wasn't the case? Perhaps they were on vacation or tied up with a major project. Regardless of the real reason, your imagination fills in the gaps. In other words, without having factual information, your thinking generates reality for you. The situation is complicated because new reality always has an emotional content. That emotional content is sometimes ugly as you experience anxiety or frustration that can accompany the imagined reasons the prospect didn't call back.

You're not going to stop your imagination from filling the information gaps. Nor are you going to stop the emotional reactions that occur as the result of your imagination's work. The best you can do is to control your imagination after it starts doing its work. Knowing that the information your imagination creates is not always factual is the cue for you to take control. Discount your imagination by telling yourself to not make assumptions and instead focus on obtaining factual information. Then divert your attention to something that is much more positive.

– 62 –

Fear is a darkroom where
negatives are developed.

– 63 –

The customer's perception of you is more important than your perception of you

Perception is reality . . . or is it? What does the following figure tell you about perception? Perceptions may fool you, but they're still your reality.

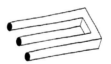

You think you're friendly, and your prospect thinks you're grumpy. Or, more important, you think you're doing everything possible to meet the prospect's needs, but he doesn't think so. Who is right? Of course, the prospect is. Doesn't sound fair, does it? But that's reality.

We recognize that the title of this chapter is not a sound mental health principle, but the perception you share with others during a sales presentation becomes their reality. The problem is you're on the wrong side of your prospect's eyeballs to see what he sees. But that doesn't leave you helpless.

Initially, it's your responsibility to *show* the prospect that you're jumping through hoops to *exceed* (not meet) their needs. You learned how to do that in Sales 101. At the risk of stating something you already know, we're going to discuss the basic sales behaviors that show your prospects that you care about meeting their needs. Consider these reminders.

Spend considerable time and energy asking the right questions to learn what the prospect needs and what he wants the product or service he's buying to do for him or his company. Refrain from letting your ego get in the way and overpower the prospect with your knowledge and all the excellent testimonials your client friends have shared with you. You're interviewing the prospect—ask questions, shut up, listen, and repeat this sequence. Ask the prospect if it's okay to take notes, and then do so.

During the interview, demonstrate that you are a keen listener by periodically paraphrasing what you've heard, for example, "Let me be certain that I understand what you are saying." Be careful to not overuse paraphrasing, or you'll give the impression of not being sincere—that would not be a good thing! Once you've completed this phase of the selling process, repeat the needs defined by the client and what he wants the product or service to do. Now ask the prospect a very important question: "It's important that I fully understand your needs for me to hit your target. Is there anything else I *need* to know or can do to understand fully?" Now you are trying to get on the other side of your prospect's eyeballs to see what he sees. You may offer suggestions of what you can do, for example, talk to those who are using an existing product or service, or see what the prospect's company is currently doing. You get the picture.

Now you're at a choice point. Do you ask for another meeting now that you've had time to process the information you learned, or do you proceed with your sales presentation? The answer to that question may depend upon several factors: what the dollar size of the sale is, whether you need input from additional company personnel, what type of proposal is necessary, et cetera. If you do schedule a follow-up meeting, ask for permission to call if you should have additional questions. Of course you're going to have additional questions. You want to show the prospect that you're doing everything you can to both understand and meet his needs and wants.

– 64 –

Relationships are all there is.

— 65 —
When you're being driven nuts

W hat in the world is wrong with that guy? Why is he calling again?"

You're going to have clients and client situations that drive you nuts. When that client calls or the nutty situation occurs, it stimulates a chain of events that may not be healthy for a successful working relationship with the client. Kerry Patterson, Joseph Grenny, Ron McMillan, and Al Switzler highlighted this series of frustrating events in their best-selling book, *Crucial Confrontations: Tools for Resolving Broken Promises, Violated Expectations, and Bad Behavior.*

See and hear > Tell a story > Feel > Act

When your problem client leaves yet another voicemail, your overactive imagination interprets the situation as an ugly story in lightning speed. For example, "I've told them how to use their new software until I'm blue in the face. Why can't they learn it?" In spite of the fact that assuming quite often leads you to the wrong conclusion, you do it anyway. Doing so seems to be human nature and is usually a waste of energy.

The problem is the story created by your imagination leads to ugly feelings like frustration, and that in turn leads to acting on this emotion. You're tempted to call and tell the client, "%@&*"! Calling at this point could be a mistake because your frustration could bleed into the conversation. According to Patterson et. al., acting in an unprofessional manner never wins you points.

You need to stop and get control. The first step to do this is being aware of the automatic response to interpret a reason for a telephone call. The second step is being aware of the powerful and potentially adverse impact your imagination has upon you. The third step is stopping the snowball effect that occurs when you allow your imagination to run wild.

The antidote is to act exactly the opposite of how you feel. To do that, you must change your thoughts. You can do that by listing positive reasons the client may have called. She wants to thank you for all the work you've done. She wants to let you know that everything is now working beautifully. Perhaps she wants to offer you a referral. Or, on the other hand, this could be another opportunity to learn how to respond to another frustrating situation. Thinking about the positive consequences can create a more positive emotional state. Thus, you can achieve your goal to exhibit a positive action.

Even as you think of the positive reasons the client called, your imagination wants to argue with you, and the internal struggle begins as you start to think that's not the real reason they're calling. Stop the argument. You're going to assume the content is positive until proven otherwise.

The timing of your call to deal with the emotionally laden situation can also help you. If you've got excellent self-control, then you can return the call with some positive greeting: "John, I bet you're calling to tell me that the system is working just like it was designed—am I right?" Another possibility is to make the call when you're feeling really optimistic and filled with positive energy. You already know you'll have to make calls that require as much positive energy as you can muster.

For the sake of this topic, let's assume you're dealing with a series of calls on the same issue. Instead of allowing your imagination to immediately put the caller into the RDC (really dumb client) category, let's exert control and approach it from a root-cause analysis perspective. Let's put your imagination to work constructively. Begin by putting yourself in the customer's shoes and imagine the frustration they're experiencing. Tell them you know they're frustrated and you want to put this energy to work to solve the problem. Meet with the client for an out-of-the-box problem-solving session. Conduct a brainstorming session to list all the possible causes of the problem. Upon completing a comprehensive list, consider the validity each could contribute to the cause of the problem. Then, of course, you're going to start acting on your conclusions and babysit the situation until it's resolved.

Your objective is to make the pain-in-the-neck customer into a loyal one as a result of the excellent service you've provided. Actually, that happens more often than not because you've demonstrated your ability to take care of the customer when you really want the fight-or-flight instinct to control your reaction.

Then, of course, you may always have a client you would like to fire. That's the subject of Thing 67.

— 66 —

There will never be a traffic jam
for those going the extra mile.

− 67 −
I would like to fire my client

Personality conflicts often leave you wishing you could fire the client. Very few salespeople, though, have that luxury.

We're back to the cause-and-effect relationship between the incident and your imagination, feelings, and actions introduced in the previous chapter. The natural tendency is to allow the frustration generated by the different personalities to bubble over into the working relationship. These situations beg you to exert self-control and rise above the situation instead of climbing into the gutter with the conflict.

Examine the differences that contribute to frustration. I—Larry—worked with a company whose CEO was analytical, and he surrounded himself with analytical team members. Considerable frustration was the result of my being more assertive than this team and much less detail-oriented. I understood the reasons for the frustrating working relationship. That understanding made the conflict easier to understand but didn't remove it. I continued to think they demanded more documentation than necessary, and the process moved at a snail's pace instead of as fast as a roadrunner.

Fortunately, in this case, I found several interests I had in common with various members of the team. Discussing these interests helped to establish the rapport necessary for an effective working relationship. Several team members eventually became good friends.

I also emphasized the progress made within the organization. I knew the work had a positive impact upon more people than just the executive team. Helping people become successful is always a good thing.

In summary, when you feel like firing your client, understand what is driving a wedge into the working relationship. If you must continue working with the client, then start looking for common interests and focus on the successes. You receive what you share with others, and you'll feel better when focusing on the positive characteristics of the working relationship.

— 68 —

When you start taking your customers for granted, you start losing them.

– 69 –
What do I do now?

All of us have been in selling situations in which we've been misinterpreted, resulting in our sales presentation getting derailed. I—Larry—made the comment during a sales presentation that billions of dollars are wasted on training activities because most companies don't implement an accountability system to ensure a transfer of learning. One of my prospects angrily exclaimed, "You're saying that our sales training program is not producing excellent salespeople?" Sometimes you're going to walk into a land mine. My statement was true, but it obviously touched a hot button, and the sales presentation was at a very critical point. How do you recover from such a blunder? Or do you let it go south, take your lumps, and go home? One of the participants in that meeting later explained that the person behind the angry explosion was one of the creators of the company's learning and development process.

When the land mine explodes, try to recover.

First, immediately state what you didn't want to convey. In my case, I could have said, "Thanks, Michael, for bringing that concern to my attention. I did not mean to imply that your training program does not have a lot of content or is not effective. I'm sure you've included the information that your salespeople need to be successful for your company."

Second, explain what you *do* mean. Let's continue with my example. I could've strengthened my comments by providing a more thorough explanation: "Most companies use the 'throw-the-mud-against-the-wall-and-hope-some-of-it-sticks' principle. To maximize the financial investment to present the training opportunity, companies need to implement a follow-up accountability system to ensure that the training transferred to the workplace. In your case, I know that you track pre- and post-sales of every training event."

In my case, I was encouraging the prospect to add an additional accountability system to measure behavior change and the effectiveness of the supervisor's working relationship to improve sales performance. In this particular instance, I could've asked a question like, "If I could show you an accountability system that is a natural extension of your existing accountability system that also maximizes the return on your financial investment, would you be interested?"

It can be difficult to think on your feet during the heat of the sales presentation. This is why it's important to add another element to your training program: create difficult scenarios and rehearse the script you want on the tip of your tongue when difficult situations present themselves. You want to practice every challenging situation until each solicits your automatic recovery response.

$-$ 70 $-$
Work your butt off, then enjoy the rewards

Thomas Edison offers sage advice that at first glance may appear as an oxymoron: "Everything comes to him who hustles while he waits." Edison reminds us to have confidence that we will receive the fruits of our labor, that our success is in direct proportion to how hard we work.

World-class performers are willing to do whatever needs to be done, including what other performers do not do. World-class performers fully expect their preparations to result in success. You want to do the same: put your nose to the grindstone, preparing for your eventual success. Do what you must do to master the details that eventually drive success. Step out of your comfort zone to practice those activities you find uncomfortable but that are likewise important to your success. Feeling the discomfort associated with stepping out of your comfort zone is the only way to continue learning the self-confidence necessary to underwrite your successful career.

Edison is also reminding you to focus on being the best version of you and creating success for your team and company. Too often, success is equated to the number of dollar bills in your pocket. Money will find you when you focus on being a world-class salesperson because becoming the best version of you is the right thing to do.

— 71 —

Always ask for the order. Don't worry about your technique or style.

— 72 —

Have a single, consolidated planning calendar that you keep with you at all times.

— 73 —
Respect

Respect is another very important sales relationship value that can be difficult to define. Ask several people in your office to define respect. Do you think their answers would match yours? Try it to see.

Respecting a prospect shows that you value them as an individual. Respect is what every prospect wants. Sometimes the prospect doesn't get it from inside their organization, but you can be certain they want it from you. Let's define a blueprint of showing your prospect respect.

1. Treat them as a professional

Recognize your prospect as a professional. You're going to meet some prospects and wonder how in the world they got their job. Quickly banish these thoughts because your behaviors can automatically reflect such thoughts. That can be the kiss of death to your sales call.

In spite of what you're looking at, think of your prospect as a professional.

2. Recognize they're knowledgeable

I—Larry—was part-owner of a preemployment testing service. I happened to attend a sales call with two of my company's salespeople. I just melted with embarrassment during the sales presentation. For some reason, one of the employees took the sales presentation as an opportunity to educate the prospect about the laws regulating drug testing. The prospect simply sat there looking helpless. It was not a pretty scene.

It's perfectly okay to recognize education gaps and offer assistance to provide necessary information, but acting like the prospect is stupid (despite what you may think) is not going to win you any points.

3. Show you're interested

Show the prospect you're interested in him as an individual. This can be tricky because you've got to be able to read their social style. You show interest in the Driver who is driven by getting results by showing how to get results and helping him be a winner. The Expressive wants you to be enthusiastic, energetic, and an interesting conversationalist. It's important to show the Amiable that you're interested in him as a person. The Analytical wants you to show him that you're interested in helping him be correct and make the right decisions through showing him accurate data.

4. Ask questions

At the risk of being redundant, we've got to mention the importance of asking diagnostic questions to learn specific needs and desired benefits. The last thing you want to do is to leave the impression you understand when the prospect believes you don't. Show interest by ensuring that you understand his needs and desired benefits. Asking the following question shows respect: "It's important that I fully understand your needs for me to hit your target. Is there anything else I need to know or can do to understand fully?"

5. Use input

Show the prospect how their valuable input helped you to customize your product or service to meet their need or achieve the desired benefits. Showing prospects how their input assisted you sends the very important psychological message that they are valued.

6. Show appreciation

Win, lose, or draw, show the prospect you appreciate everything they did to assist your efforts to help them be successful via purchasing your product or service. Losing is not fun. Losing often elicits ugly thoughts, which frequently lead to ugly behaviors. Remember the sage advice of Byrd's quote: "If you're going to burn a bridge, you better be able to walk on water in the future."

— 74 —
The Ph.D. of sales

Preserve
Human
Dignity

To put this tip into practical terms, be kind to everyone!

― 75 ―

"When we change the way we look at things, things change the way they look."
—Dr. Wayne Dyer

Confidently thinking you're right can be both a blessing and a curse. It's important to show prospects your confidence, because they will feel more confident about your ability to assist them. As we've said before, you receive what you share with others.

Your confidence should always be a blessing. That blessing can be challenged during times when you think you're dead right, and you're dead wrong. There are certain behavioral characteristics you need to exhibit to continue to use your confidence as a blessing.

1. Open mind

You want to approach every situation with an open mind. That means to objectively review the facts of the situation, which serve as the basis for the decision. If you're one of those stubborn, strong-willed, "my-way" thinkers, being open-minded can be a challenge. You may trick yourself into thinking that you're open-minded because you base decisions on facts, but generally you're the one who declares the set of facts you consider important. When you blind yourself from the truth, your confidence is a curse.

Even a blind hog will find an acorn occasionally. You want to open your mind to see all the acorns and make winning easier. Consider the consequences of being blinded by your own confidence when you are dead wrong but believe you're dead right. Not only does that sabotage making the best decisions, but think about the messages that you're sending to your prospects and those working with you. Hopefully, being a "my-way" thinker (being stubborn) is not your desired reputation. Also, be aware of the fine line that separates confidence and arrogance. Arrogance is a kiss of death.

2. Understanding before being understood

Stephen Covey offers wise advice with his principle of understanding: with your open mind, you want to strive to understand all the facts of the situation. Approach the subject recognizing that you want to make the best decision regardless of the owner of that decision. While considering the facts, take advantage of the principle that *you find what you're looking for.* Thus, look for what you can learn to improve the decision, and you'll find it.

The second half of Covey's principle encourages you to offer what you think after understanding all the facts. Confident "my-way" thinkers typically make statements similar to "This is what I think needs to be done." That statement can be a turnoff to people, especially if it continues to reinforce your reputation of thinking only one way. Instead, introduce your opinions in a question format. For example, "What do you think would happen if . . . ?" The question format softens the blow while still achieving your goal to put your idea on the table.

3. Flexibility

Exhibit your confidence by admitting your original position was wrong based on understanding the facts of the situation. Being humble is a sign of confidence. Based on your new reality, things change, just as Dyer suggests. Based on your new perception, it's time to be flexible.

We hope we've achieved our goal to encourage you to be the person who is constantly asking, "Am I looking at every situation through the best set of eyes?"

When something comes up, let them know as soon as you can

If you're in sales long enough, you'll have bad news the prospect is not going to like: "The manufacturing plant messed up the order"; "The product has to be re-run"; and "The expected delivery is postponed another three days." You've spent months working to get this client. It's their first order, and you promised to meet their deadline. Your credibility is on the line.

Your frustration boils, and you want to wring the plant manager's neck. Everyone knew the sensitivity of this order. The plant has been hungry for new business, and finally there's an opportunity to show what you can do. And then this occurs. You feel that if you didn't have bad luck, you would have no luck at all.

Your pleasure-pain instinctual response tempts you to postpone making the call to the client. As you ponder the situation, remember that trust is the lubricant of working relationships. Dependability and keeping people informed with the facts are touchstones for creating trust. In this scenario, dependability has been shot because someone misread the order sheet, so quality control did not catch it in time to meet the original deadline. At best, you can deliver a partial order.

Under these dire circumstances, it's important to exhibit one element of trust and inform the new client ASAP. Who makes the call? Do you or the plant manager possess the verbal skills to participate in a conference call with the client?

Under these circumstances, it's tempting to lay all the blame on the manufacturing facility. But what message does the blame game send to the client? You don't want that. What's another option?

Whether it's you or you and the plant manager,

exhibit the courage to do what must be done. Honesty is always the best policy. Make that call. Tell the client you wanted her to know ASAP that the worst possible scenario has happened. Human error caused manufacturing errors, and it's not possible to ship the full order by the expected delivery date even with the plant running overtime. Everyone feels terrible for obvious reasons. The schedule is to deliver the remainder of the order three days late. Hopefully, our human error is not going to cause a major delay for the client. Finally, if your company is customer-service oriented, you can ask the client what you can do to make it right for her. In other words, what can be done for you to have a second opportunity to show the capability of your manufacturing plant?

We know it sounds like manipulation, but you want to play to the client's emotions. The client understands human error. She doesn't like them either, but she's had her share of them. She understands the uncomfortable position you're in. Demonstrating the confidence to work out this delicate situation can actually show the client that you have the exact personality characteristics that she likes to work with. This is an opportunity to show everyone you have the "right stuff."

— 77 —

Eating your elephants one bite at a time

You've got two proposals to write, ten voice-mails, an untold number of e-mails, ten customers to call to ensure they're satisfied with their recent purchases, a list your sales manager just gave you of another twenty prospects to call within the next two days, and an errand from your spouse to pick up a couple of items on the way home. So where do you start eating this elephant?

1. Attitude

Thinking "there is no way I can get all of this done" puts you into a trap that you don't want to be in. If you truly believe that, then shut the office door and go home. That attitude is not the pathway to success. Remember, you always find what you look for, so it matters not how large the elephant may appear. You approach it with a "yes, I can eat it" attitude. Look for the time to get everything done, and you'll find the time.

To help you swallow, realize that this day is going to provide ample opportunities to practice maintaining a positive attitude and remaining emotionally calm, and that another day will be spent juggling priorities. The more time you're wasting fretting over the situation, the more valuable time and emotional energy you're expending that can be better spent elsewhere.

2. Priorities

One thing is certain: you can't do everything at once. Can you prioritize the tasks in terms of money-making activities and the few items that absolutely have to get done today? If so, that would be an excellent starting point.

3. Scheduling time

Schedule each priority on your calendar. You're probably laughing as you think about the ridiculousness of this suggestion. You probably have a history of trashing your to-do lists. Our point is to begin the day with a plan.

While scheduling, ensure that you put your high-payoff activities at the top of the list. For example, write down the three customers you need to communicate with today who hold the greatest chance of sales success. Don't wait until the end of the day when you're tired and don't have the magnetic sales energy required to connect with customers. Schedule tasks requiring quality quiet time in the morning or evening or while flying to your next appointment (as was done when writing this part of the book).

4. One bite at a time

Okay, while chewing the bite, savor its flavor, and focus on the pure enjoyment of successfully chewing to the point of swallowing it with a bit of wine! Focus on enjoying the process and completing each task. Take pride in your work. We know, we know—you would if you had enough time!

5. Crisis

Okay, time to throw the previous suggestions out the window, because the next crisis just walked through the door. You're at a choice point. Does the interruption constitute an emergency that needs to be handled *right now?* If so, then juggle accordingly. If not, place it in your "to be scheduled" list and continue with your list.

6. Reward

Enjoy marking the completed task off your list. At the end of the day, be proud of successfully completing tasks and maintaining a positive and calm demeanor. Avoid the temptation to beat yourself up

with the parts of the elephant you did not get to eat
today.

7. Why do I want to wake up tomorrow?

Before closing those eyelids this evening to enter
your dream state, think about the reasons you want
to wake up in the morning. Include the benefits associated with continuing to eat the elephant and practicing to become the best version of you.

— 78 —

If it can't eat you, don't worry about it.

– 79 –
What business are you in?

We've asked thousands of employees, "What business are you in?" How would you answer that question as a salesperson? The typical answers include manufacturing, health care, financial services—the technical aspects of their businesses. Let's ask a couple other questions: What would you have without customers? Or, What would you do without the people operating the manufacturing or service-delivery aspects of your business? You're right, nothing. You're in the people business. Your success depends upon working relationships with people. On a more personal level, you need other people just to survive in this world. We don't mean to burst any of your bubbles, but we do want you to face the reality of the importance of people in your life.

Customer service from the inside out

It is crucial to be the person with whom people like to work. On the one hand, you've got the internal customers, and on the other, your external customers. You're sandwiched between two sets of very important people, both determining your success. Feeling helpless yet?

Let's start with your internal customers. Typical complaints about salespeople include:

- They need to check with us before they promise unrealistic delivery schedules.
- How in the world does he expect us to meet those specifications?
- He never seems to understand that we have other salespeople and other customers who need consideration.
- He thinks he's the only person in this company.
- . . . and the list goes on.

There are basic working relationship values, such as communication, respect, trust, and teamwork, that you can use to maximize your working relationships with your internal customers. We've listed what are generally the more critical behaviors for each of these values:

1. Keep them informed when something comes up that's out of the ordinary *(communication)*.
2. Treat the internal customers as professionals. Like you, they want to be recognized for their product knowledge and capabilities to be peak performers *(respect)*.
3. Be dependable and meet or exceed their expectations *(trust)*.
4. Help them to be successful by making their jobs as easy as possible *(teamwork)*.

Note that these behaviors do not require you to learn new values or do things beyond your capability. These are already included in your behavioral library. You just need to put them to work consistently.

Consider another question: Who are you most apt to assist—someone you like or don't like? Remember, your internal customers are people, and they feel exactly the same as you. You want to be their favorite salesperson for numerous reasons, the most important being that external customer service begins with internal customer service.

External customer service

We know that you want to exceed all of your customers' expectations. Begin this section by re-reading the above behavioral blueprint while thinking about your external customers. We don't mean to oversimplify either working relationship, but you can maximize the working relationship with both customer sets with the same basic behaviors.

Jan Carlzon introduced the "Moments of Truth" concept in his best-selling book of the same name.

Carlzon encourages you to identify the significant points of customer interaction, at least the 20 percent that produce the reputation of providing excellent customer service. Develop a service strategy—how you want to manage each of these moments to exceed your customers' expectations.

Another strategy is to use the "what if" principle. Identify what can go wrong with these crucial moments of truth, and develop follow-up strategies so you can move to automatic responses if your worst nightmares become realities. Just be prepared.

Providing extra value

Frustration is going to creep into every working relationship, and each party will eventually be the guilty one. We want you to *use frustration as your best friend* as a cue to improve working relationships and add extra value to them. What can you do to take advantage of the frustration? Include either or both sets of customers in that conversation as is appropriate.

– 80 –
Don't quit before the blessing

How can Abraham Lincoln's life's history help you become a better sales professional? Study the summary of his significant life events listed below.

- He failed in business in 1831.
- He was defeated for state legislature in 1832.
- He tried another business in 1833. It failed.
- His fiancée died in 1835.
- He had a nervous breakdown in 1836.
- In 1843 he ran for Congress and was defeated.
- He tried again in 1848 and was defeated again.
- He tried running for the Senate in 1855. He lost.

- The next year he ran for vice-president and lost.
- In 1858 he ran for Senate again and was defeated again.
- Finally, in 1860, he was elected the 16th president of the United States!

What would the average person do in these circumstances? You're right, yield to defeat and focus on being a lawyer instead of a politician. Lincoln's life history provides a valuable lesson to all of us: don't quit before the blessing.

As a sales professional, you're going to face numerous obstacles—and a bunch of "no's"—on the path to becoming your best. At the time of writing this, we also received a "no" instead of the "yes" that we expected pertaining to a major contract. In spite of the initial disappointment, we had to focus on every "no" being a stepping stone to hearing the next "yes." The title of Harold Kushner's classic book, *When Bad Things Happen to Good People,* sums it up. During the bad times, we must take a lesson from Lincoln's life and maintain the optimistic attitude of expecting the best instead of accepting the tombstone of defeat.

— 81 —

Face what you fear, and what you fear will ultimately disappear.

– 82 –
Three keys to growth

1. You must go deep to grow great *(self-aware-ness)*.
2. You must let go to grow *(change your bad habits)*.
3. Greatness takes time to grow *(patience)*.

83

Self-awareness is a key building block for your sales career

One problem with our education system is that it doesn't teach us the skill sets needed to be successful! Where did you learn the selling process? Or why and how did you acquire the interpersonal skills to successfully work with prospects and use the technical process of selling? And perhaps more important, why and how did you develop the self-awareness? These crucial determinants of your success are unfortunately left to chance. We hope you agree that's not a good thing.

Self-awareness is a crucial building block. It's imperative to know who you are, especially to know your strengths and weaknesses. Honest self-awareness helps you understand the importance of being good enough to know that you're not good enough.

In other words, the more you know, the more you realize that you don't know. Self-awareness is the foundation of your continued self-improvement.

The origin of your self-awareness is open to debate. One thought is that it is DNA-determined. Consequently, you either have the gene to be self-aware, or you don't. This hypothesis sounds a bit fatalistic, don't you agree? To our knowledge, scientists have not discovered this lack-of-self-awareness gene.

Another suggested contributing factor to develop self-awareness is that you must experience a crucible. That is, you must experience a severe test or a life-changing event. In support of this hypothesis, you probably have experienced a life-changing event such as a death, loss of employment, a divorce, or health challenges. The downside of that hypothesis is, Do you need to wait until you experience such a severe ordeal to learn to be self-aware? And where does the impact of positive life-changing experiences fit into the self-awareness formula?

It's a fact that negative experiences have a longer-lasting impact than positive ones. Just consider the impact of someone who's behaved in a manner that destroyed your trust versus individuals who have acted in ways to continue to be trustworthy. Which one has the greater impact? There are a couple of explanations for the greater impact of negative experiences versus positive ones. Some writers believe that you're hardwired to think negatively because of your survival instincts. In other words, something like wondering what's wrong has helped generations of people stay alive. We think you agree that's important.

Another reason is that pain's intensity grabs your attention more so than pleasure's intensity does. In other words, the impact of pain outweighs the positive energy of a good experience, and we tend to remember the pain over the pleasurable memory of the *positive* experience. It's sad, but this is just how most people react to situations.

All this leads us to wonder whether one can learn to become self-aware. Think about this. Your body is designed to give you essential feedback. When you place an object in your hand, you can accurately describe the object without actually looking at it based on the feedback obtained through your nervous system. The nervous system helps you to become physically aware. On the other hand, your emotions constitute your psychological nervous system. Your thoughts and beliefs trigger your emotions, which are critical sources of information for self-awareness.

You want to become as acutely aware of your psychological environment as you are of your physical environment. To do so requires hard work, but we believe you'll find that the benefits of being self-aware far outweigh the work required to learn this essential skill. You can engage in a couple of exercises to help you become more self-aware.

Dr. Phil McGraw, in his best-selling book *Self Matters: Creating Your Life from the Inside Out,* suggests examining the critical experiences, decisions made, and people who've impacted your life. Once you identify these life events, record the positive and negative impacts these have had upon your life. In turn, this examination will help develop self-awareness.

Learn to be in the present. Become more aware of your thoughts and feelings as you react to events in both your internal and external worlds. Be *okay* with what you learn about yourself. After all, you are learning about you, which should be a favorite subject matter.

Your ultimate goal is to know your strengths and weaknesses and be comfortable with them. Just like a sponge changes as it absorbs water, you become a different person through your ongoing learning.

For just a moment, compare yourself with an individual who does not follow the suggestions listed in this chapter. Their blind spots—those things they don't know but others do—derail their careers. We think you will agree that that's not a desirable future.

We encourage you instead to be a student of self-awareness.

84

Selling is the university of life

Why does your company exist? Why are you employed by the company? The traditional answer is that you exist to make money for the company, and the company exists to make money for its stockholders.

We're encouraging you to rethink these traditional answers. Consider that every day is rich with opportunities to improve both the technical skills and people skills required for you to be successful. Your company's success is dependent upon *you being successful first.*

Consider that today is another day in the classroom. Every day you are practicing both the technical characteristics and interpersonal skills essential to becoming a sales professional. What better university setting to learn how to maximize your potential than your career? There is none. You have to make the decision that you're going to use today to practice the skill sets that have helped you reach your current success level—or you can raise the bar and practice an improved skill set. Without a conscious decision to practice improving your skill sets, by default, you're going to practice what you've always done, and with that, you can always expect the same results.

Life's lessons

Your sales career teaches you several critical lessons that lead to a higher quality of life.

1. Being assertive enough to ask prospects for the order is a cornerstone to enjoying life. You're consistently experiencing situations in which you need to take charge, for example, negotiating purchases, managing your health care, and working with other service providers

to you and your family. Being assertive helps you take control of your life.

2. Interpersonal skills are required to strengthen your relationships with prospects and customers. These help you work better with all of the lives that you touch.

3. You've learned to be more optimistic and look for the good in spite of the propensity to focus on the negative. Research shows that optimistic people lead healthier lives and can more quickly bounce back to adjust to life's many frustrations and disappointments. As you know, frustrations and disappointments tend to dominate all aspects of your life. Your optimism helps you find the good in these experiences rather than being victimized by them.

4. You've learned the critical success factor that will keep your eyes locked on your goal. You'll have many goals in your life that will require this same skill in order to achieve them.

5. People, whether they realize it or not, are constantly selling themselves, change, and other ideas to their employers, family, and friends. You have a distinct advantage because you know how to use selling skills in these situations.

6. Last, but certainly not least, identifying your life's purpose provides direction and meaning for everything you do. Your life's purpose is core to maximizing the many gifts life has to offer.

In closing this chapter, it is important to note that you now have critical skill sets to teach your family and other people you touch. You're in the position to help others maximize what life has to offer.

85

Bury your ego. Don't be the star. Be the star maker!
— *Bud Hadfield*

The last thing you want your prospects or customers to say about you is, "There is one egotistical salesperson!"

Your ego is a definite asset. Your self-confidence is the energy source that keeps you selling. Without the self-confidence to sell, you would have a different career. Too much self-confidence, though, turns into arrogance. When that happens, self-confidence looks like conceit and self-importance—thus, it's all about you instead of the prospect or client. As illustrated below, you must be aware of the fine line that separates confidence from being egotistical.

Lack of Self-Confidence	Confident	Egotistical

David Marcum and Steven Smith suggest an ideal state of humility in their best-selling book, *Egonomics: What Makes Ego Our Greatest Asset (Or Most Expensive Liability)*. As you may recall, these authors describe that ideal state as " We, then me," "I'm brilliant, and I'm not," and " One more thing," all described in detail in Chapter 9.

Controlling your ego

As one client recently stated, "It's important to put your ego in your back pocket." Let's address how to do that.

1. Practice humility. As previously discussed, it would be nice if a healthy dose of humility was genetically "fixed," but that appears not to be the case. Instead, you must learn to be humble. Refresh your memory on what humility means by flipping back to Chapter 9.

2. Know your strengths and limitations. Know who you are. Be proud of your strengths and openly accept your weaknesses. You show acceptance of you by admitting your limitations and doing the same with your mistakes.

3. Be comfortable in your skin. Remember, you were a person before being in your present position. If you wrap your self-esteem around your position, title, or the initials following your name, you're in trouble.

4. Realize that everyone is equally important. Read this sentence: Rxmxmbxr that xvxy lxxtxr of thx alphabxt is xqually important to makx a sxntxncx xasily rxad. Like the letters of the alphabet, every person you meet is equally important.

5. Appreciate others. Give credit to others for your successes, and accept responsibilities for mistakes. Show appreciation to everyone in your prospects' and customers' offices as well as to your internal customers. These people are helping you succeed. Show them your appreciation. And remember, the number one want of people is to be appreciated.

6. Help others be successful. As we've stressed, you receive what you share with others. Thus, the more people you help be successful, the more successful you become.

7. Practice gentleness. Show the "kinder, softer, more tender" aspects of your personality. When you do this, you're putting other people first.

Now that you've got a behavioral blueprint to keep your ego in control, go forth and be humbly self-confident.

─ 86 ─

It's harder to keep an account than it was to get it.

– 87 –
Self-confidence

Self-confidence is critical to a successful sales career. Your "I can" attitude gives you the energy to do what you do every day. In some respects, your sales career would be easier if your DNA gave you the self-confidence necessary to guarantee success. But life doesn't work that way. You get it the old-fashioned way—you must work for it. Fortunately, it is one of the natural resources waiting to be used, and you can have as much of it as you want.

You learn self-confidence through changing. We want you to think of change as an energy system. That is, some energy sources encourage you to change while others encourage you to remain as is. You must manage your energy systems.

Learning self-confidence begins with your comfort zone, which consists of those activities you feel comfortable doing. The middle of your comfort zone includes habits that are second nature to you. As you extend toward the perimeter, the activities may be a bit more challenging, but you do them anyway (for example, calling on certain prospects). Those lying outside of the comfort zone—e.g., cold calling—

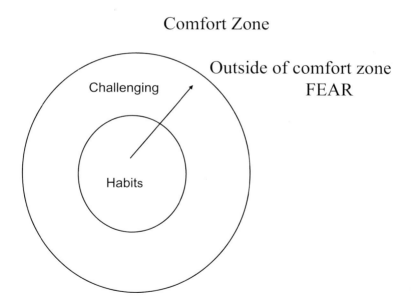

Comfort Zone

Challenging

Habits

Outside of comfort zone
FEAR

represent the rich learning opportunities to continue learning self-confidence. We've illustrated the content of this paragraph in the following figure.

Learning self-confidence extends the perimeter of your comfort zone, and you learn it by stepping outside of your comfort zone. To do that, you must *Feel the Fear and Do It Anyway,* the title of Susan Jeffers's best-selling book. To help you, use frustration as your friend. That is, list the advantages and disadvantages of your current behavior, such as not making cold calls. You want the intensity of the disadvantages of not making cold calls to be great enough to help make the decision that remaining the same is not an option. As illustrated in the following figure, you want this energy to push you out of the comfort zone.

Next, you want a strong magnetic force to pull you out of the comfort zone by listing the advantages

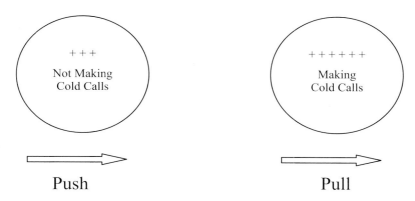

Push   Pull

and disadvantages of making cold calls. By combining the push and the pull, you can readily see the force to change and develop self-confidence.

Because of the phenomenon referred to as resistance to change, you know that change is not that easy. You may look at resistance as a negative event because of the discomfort that's usually associated with it. With that perspective, you're creating a temptation to resist the resistance by staying the same. As shown in the following figure, there is no denying the opposite forces created when you resist change.

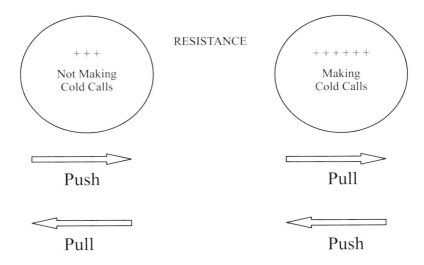

RESISTANCE

Not Making Cold Calls

Making Cold Calls

Push

Pull

Pull

Push

The forces of resistance can provide a very strong temptation for you to remain locked into your comfort zone. You have to manage this internal struggle to increase the intensity of the energy sources that encourage you to change. You can do that.

We're encouraging you to view resistance to change as a positive, natural part of the change process. Your body is telling you that you're changing, which is exactly what you want to do. Plus, you're learning self-confidence, getting stronger, and advancing your career. This is the positive power of the pain of change.

The antidote to override the forces that keep you locked in your comfort zone is to keep your eyes locked onto your goal while reviewing the disadvantages of not making cold calls combined with the advantages of making the calls. The magnetic pull associated with the advantages of successfully making cold calls will ultimately be the force that helps you change. Remember, it is easier to pull a rope than it is to push it.

We like to contrast the behavior of a turtle versus that of a squirrel. The turtle extends its neck from its comfort zone—the shell—to begin walking across the road. Upon hearing an approaching car, it quickly withdraws into its comfort zone. Just as quickly, it continues on its journey with the passing of the car. Contrast that with the squirrel that quickly darts into the road. Upon hearing the advancing car, it becomes confused and eventually darts back to the side of the road (its comfort zone). That decision is frequently a fatal one. There is true danger in the comfort zone!

So when the going gets tough, do you tend to act like a turtle or a squirrel? The temptation is to be the squirrel, but you want to be the turtle.

Self-confidence grows each time you walk across that imaginary line—the perimeter of your comfort zone—created by your imagination. Ever so slowly, you show yourself that you can successfully walk across this line, and then the self-imposed resistance created by your imagination dissipates.

"Low self-esteem is like driving through life with your hand brake on." —*Maxwell Maltz*

Your self-esteem may be the most important topic of this book. The essence of self-esteem is the degree to which you like yourself. It differs slightly from self-confidence, which is the "I can do" attitude. You may have self-confidence yet not have positive self-esteem. Of course, the reverse is also true.

With the exception of genetics, you're born with a blank page on which your program is written. When you are young, you're like a sponge, absorbing the positive and negative events that occur in your life. As you mature, you eventually interpret experiences through your self-esteem glasses. The end result is a combination of memories that contribute to either a negative or positive self-esteem—what you ultimately believe about yourself.

To complicate matters, a negative self-esteem is very resistant to change. The good news is that it can be improved, and it's definitely worth the work to do so. Numerous books have been written on this subject (Google "Nathaniel Brandon"), and we could write one as well. However, the essence of this relearning process is to concentrate on your successes and your other positive attributes. The other half of the formula is to learn from the failures and other negative experiences and then let them go by forgiving yourself. Your thoughts control your feelings, so that explains the importance of controlling your thoughts. We also know that controlling your thoughts is easier said than done. For one thing, you can't control all of them all of the time. The negative ones occur spontaneously. You can, though, control your reaction to these negative thoughts. That is, instead of dwelling on your negative thoughts and feeling badly, take control and focus on the positive elements in your life.

Improving your self-esteem

We're listing several critical strategies that you can employ to improve your self-esteem.

1. *Know that it's okay.* The more we fight our internal struggles, the more we succumb to them. Yes, the more you fight "not feeling" badly about yourself, the more you will feel badly. Thus, you want to accept your level of self-esteem regardless of what it is. That's the starting point.

2. *List your assets.* List all of your positive characteristics. Review this list daily.

3. *Forgive yourself and others.* Yes, other people have said stupid things to you, and you've contributed your share of stupid acts to feel badly about, but there is no changing history. As Byrd says, "Flush it and move on." We don't like that these events happened, but they did. Your task is to learn from them and move on.

4. *Do whatever needs to be done to look nice.* This can be a touchy subject. If you're overweight, lose weight. If you're out of shape, start an exercise program. Dress nicely. Taking control of just these facets of your life will help you feel better.

5. *Define your life's purpose.* We've discussed this subject elsewhere in this book. We firmly believe that doing so will facilitate a positive self-esteem.

6. *Associate with positive people.* Take a friend inventory. Are your friends helping to promote your positive self-esteem or tear it down? You're not going to soar with the eagles if you associate with turkeys. Surround yourself with a positive support system.

7. *Don't wish you were someone else—to do so is to waste the person you are.* In this competitive world, it seems only logical to compare yourself with others. There is a strong temptation to compare yourself with those who seem

to be doing better or have more of something. That's a waste of energy, as the only person you can be is you. What's important is the progress you're making, so focus on your set of internal standards.

8. *Compliment.* When you're struggling with self-esteem issues, you don't feel as though you deserve compliments, so the natural tendency is to reject them. However, you need to accept them. And give plenty of them to yourself. At the end of the day, you want to compliment your day's successes. You've got them, and you'll find them as you start looking for them.

We wish you could control your self-esteem as easily as you turn the faucet on and off, but we know that it's not that easy. This change takes time. But trust us, it's worth the effort and time. It feels good to feel good about yourself!

237

– 89 –
I made it! My personal story

I (Larry) am the most unlikely candidate to have had a successful career in the field of sales.

To put everything into perspective, I was told that I did not have the intellectual capacity to graduate from college. I tease people that I was in the top twenty-four of my high school graduating class. Of course, there were only twenty-four of us who graduated that year!

I started my college education as a shy, introverted, insecure eighteen-year-old farm boy. To my surprise, I found college much easier than I expected, and circumstances led me to obtain a Ph.D. in psychology. Let's fast-forward to 1989. I had just completed five very difficult years. Boredom pushed me to leave a successful career as CEO of a mental health center. Following a brief stint as a VP of a marketing firm and another two years in the mental health field, I finalized my personal mission statement that focused on helping people. With that in hand, I launched my management consulting company in January of that year.

The challenges were immediate. I had enough money to survive for two months. I needed at least five consulting days per month to meet my financial obligations. It gets worse! Not having sales training, I had no clue how to sell or how hard it was to sell. Combine these realities with a lack of self-confidence, and you would have guessed that I was doomed for failure. Looking back, I'm amazed that I made it. I am a classic example that if you want something badly enough, you can make it happen.

Initially my fuel to continue was the excitement associated with being a consultant and owning my own business, which had been goals of mine for several years. Soon the realities of the world hit me square in the face, and the fear of failure became a constant companion. The possibility of failing was so strong by the end of 1989 that I was tempted to abandon my dreams and return to the boredom of full-time employment within the mental health industry.

As I look back, there is a combination of several variables that contributed to my success.

First, I had written my personal mission statement—to help people through consulting—that launched my company. In spite of all the challenges and frustrations, I knew that I was doing what I was meant to do. Selling was the necessary evil to open the door for me to do what I enjoy doing the most: teaching.

Second, I stayed locked onto my goals. Today, I still review my goal sheet daily. I begin the day thinking about my life's mission and what I want to achieve through this mission.

Third was hard work. I had the necessary self-discipline to stay focused on high-payoff activities. I practiced making cold telephone calls while driving between appointments. I wrote multiple sales scripts and practiced them until I could recite them while acting naturally.

Fourth, I celebrated the personal successes that were the result of calling prospects, making the cold calls that generated appointments, and making the sales calls that ultimately resulted in getting the order. These "small" successes were critical steps to a successful consulting career.

Needless to say, I'm grateful and feel so fortunate that I stayed focused on my purpose statement. It seemed that every time I needed an opportunity, it appeared. This book is an example of how opportunity knocks. As Byrd frequently reminds me, there are no coincidences. As with every business, I've had good years and then I've had better years. Even the slower times seemed to appear at just the right time for me to complete a major initiative. Yes, I believe there is order in the universe and that good things await those who believe.

– 90 –

"If we make each and every moment count, we will have 'enough' time." —*Amy Jones*

If all of us would have received a dollar for every time we'd heard "I don't have enough time," we could all retire. Not having enough time has to be the universal excuse for not getting things done. There is no doubt that time is a critical resource. You don't have enough time to complete your career priorities; you have the demands of family time and the demands of taking care of you. So you may consider Amy Jones's advice an oxymoron. Or is something else contributing to your time-management woes?

We could discuss the many benefits of effective time-management techniques, such as scheduling your to-do list and reading each e-mail once. But these are things that you already know. We want to introduce you to another approach to effective time-management.

Four types of energy

In their best-selling book, *The Power of Full Engagement: Managing Energy, Not Time, Is the Key to High Performance and Personal Renewal,* Jim Loehr and Tony Schwartz conclude that energy is the key to having enough time. These authors highlight the importance of four types of energy: physical, emotional, mental, and spiritual. To be fully engaged, you must be physically energized, emotionally connected, mentally focused, and spiritually aligned. Full engagement requires drawing on each of these four sources of energy. All of them are necessary, none is sufficient by itself, and each influences the others.

You may argue that you don't have enough time to keep each of these energy tanks full, and we would counter that you don't have the luxury *to not* keep them full if you expect peak performance.

1. Physical. Rest, exercise, and proper diet are key ingredients to fill this energy tank. Of these three, people complain about not having enough time to exercise. Our guess is that's just an excuse to stay a couch potato. You always feel energized after exercising. If you question that comment, we challenge you take a vigorous walk when you are feeling emotionally exhausted and experience the wonders of exercise firsthand.

2. Emotional. Have fun with your hobbies and family. I (Larry) want to start every day as a mini-vacation by doing something that I enjoy. I like to write. So I schedule one to two hours of writing time every morning. This book is a living example of these daily mini-vacations.

3. Mental. Nothing takes the place of a positive mental attitude. Fill your mind with positive information—read good books. We often hear the complaint that "I don't like to read" or "I don't have enough time to read." Then buy or check out audiobooks. Subscribing to a quote-of-the-day service provides excellent reading every morning.

Do you classify your coworkers and friends as positive-minded people? You should surround yourself with other positive-thinking people. A positive mental attitude is contagious, so you want to take advantage of that source of positive energy.

4. Spiritual. Psychologically, there is a benefit to believing in a higher power. You feel more secure when believing that a higher power is assisting you. We have no intention to enter into the debate about the existence of God (we'll leave that subject with you), but there is a funny thing about your beliefs: if you believe a higher power is assisting you, then it is.

If connecting with a higher power is not your thing, then choose to connect with the beauty of this world. Marvel at the sights and sounds of Mother Nature. You can combine enjoying nature with an energetic walk. Recently, I (Larry) had the good fortune to jog along the Columbia River in Portland,

Oregon, while looking at the snow-capped peak of Mount Hood. That was a beautiful spiritual experience. Byrd frequently enjoys a mystic oak on the banks of the Guadalupe River to help fill his emotional tanks.

The point is, when you keep your energy tanks full, you'll have the time to do whatever needs to be done.

– 91 –
Everyone needs a coach

We can hear you now: "I don't need a coach! This is selling, not an athletic event!" If you want to be better than good, we're going to ask you to rethink your point of view. If you don't care how good you are, then you probably shouldn't be reading this book.

In his book *Sell with Confidence: Unlock Your Potential,* Paul Vitale reminds us of the importance of having a sales coach. Do you think you're perfect at being a sales professional? Your answer should be "no"; a "yes" answer may suggest you have more confidence—or arrogance—than your prospect and customers want to see.

World-class professionals in search of perfection realize the importance of an objective third party to examine their performance. A new set of eyes can see the forest, while your eyes are locked onto the trees. These professionals want to identify their performance gaps or the difference between their current performance and that of the next level. We hope you want to continuously raise your performance bar.

An obvious coach is your supervisor. Helping you to become the best version of you is a critical responsibility of your supervisor. Unfortunately, many supervisors do not fulfill this responsibility for a variety of reasons, usually because it can be uncomfortable. If that's true for you, then you must accept the responsibility to find a coach.

Another workplace option is discussing the best practices with your peer group. No doubt, such discussions can be extremely helpful.

The truth of the matter is that sometimes it's just nice to talk to someone who is independent of your financial security. It's beneficial to have someone you can discuss your performance and other issues

with without worrying about them being dissemi-
nated throughout the workplace. The key is having
a coach who will tell you what you need to hear, not
necessarily what you want to hear.

− 92 −
Very important person

While dining at a well-known franchise restaurant, I (Larry) noticed the manager walking around asking customers, "How is your meal this evening?" She asked every customer the same question, including me. On the positive side, she made eye contact, but on the negative, she didn't stay around very long. Did she sound sincere? You guessed it, she sounded mechanical and rote as if she was just carrying out her duties. In retrospect, I wish I had told her "no" just to see her reaction. (A missed opportunity!)

Why do people not get it? Do they not realize that customers are not completely stupid and can see the lack of sincerity? We hope we're not describing you.

You want every customer to feel like a VIP. Life is a struggle, and too many times your customers feel beat down and frustrated from the daily grind. You can be the spark of positive energy. You want them to feel good because they've interacted with you.

Let's take our restaurant manager. I would certainly have felt her sincerity if she would have slowed down, looked me in the eye, and asked me a question about my meal that differed from the one I heard her ask the couple in the next booth. I was working on a document at the time, so she obviously knew that I was a businessperson. She could have easily asked if I was in town on business, where I was from, thanked me for dining with them, and asked me to return while bragging about another entrée that I might enjoy when I returned.

In a few minutes, I could have had a completely different perception of her than my initial one. I would return to that restaurant because the food is good, the location is convenient, and the service was fast, but I definitely will not return because of her.

You have to ask the question, "Why do you want your customers to do business with you?" Hopefully, it's because you show them they are VIPs and that your customer service exceeds their expectations. That's the slight edge that will take your sales career to the next level.

— 93 —
Never take your business relationships for granted.

94

"Obstacles are things a person sees when he takes his eyes off his goal." — *E. Joseph Cossman*

Are you aware that many accidents occur while people gawk as they drive past another accident? Our bodies follow our eyes, which cause us to steer the car toward the accident.

The road you're traveling on is filled with potholes. You'll get into a sales slump. There are days when everything you touch falls apart. It seems the success formula on a bad day reads *Success = 90 percent frustration and disappointment.* These challenges are going to tempt you to look in many different directions that may not necessarily be conducive to being a peak performing salesperson. You may even start seeing an image of defeat, but you know where that image can lead.

What do you do when challenging times stretch you? Robert Schuller offered sage advice, *"Tough times never last, but tough people do."* Let's toughen you up by reviewing the several psychological advantages of keeping your eyes on the goal.

1. To begin with, keeping your eyes on the goal energizes the natural progression to success. Mother Nature's plants and animals do what comes naturally—be all that they can be in accordance to the availability of the needed nutrients. People are part of Mother Nature, and you're equipped with the capability to think positive thoughts to advance your development. Your eyes are going to look where your thoughts direct them, so take advantage of the natural way and think those optimistic thoughts that help you stay focused on your journey.

2. As long as you can see your goal, you have "hope," the critical energy system that keeps

you going. When you lose hope, you're done!
3. Opportunities will appear on the horizon, and you'll see them.
4. Keeping your eye on the goal engages the Law of Closure. Your body strives to stay in a state of balance or homeostasis. Focusing on your goal creates tension. Your mind generates ideas to rid the body of this tension, and these ideas help you reach your goal.
5. During challenging times, you'll make the decision to fight or flight. By being true to Mother Nature and staying focused on your goals, you acquire the essential self-confidence to make a molehill out of the next mountain that you face.
6. When you make the decision to take advantage of them, obstacles can provide a rich learning opportunity.

95

"Here is a simple but powerful
rule: Always give people more
than they expect to get."
—*Nelson Boswell*

We like to think that we salespeople are independent. That may be a reason you selected a
career in sales. The truth is that you probably have
more flexibility (or should we say perks?) than other
employees, such as lunches, dinners, and golf out-
ings, to name a few. We know, you deserve them,
and they go with the territory.

But let's rethink your independence. Actually,
your success is *very* dependent upon both internal
and external customers. You're sandwiched between
two critical variables. Maybe you don't have as
much independence as you thought. You've got to

make both sets of customers happy. Boswell offers excellent advice—you make them happy by exceeding their expectations. Doing so increases the likelihood that your customers will exceed your sales expectations.

It's now the end of the day, and you're going home. As you go, take Boswell's advice with you. It can have the same positive impact with your family that it does at work. You know only too well that a happy home life has a positive impact upon working with your team members, and excellent internal customer service provides an excellent energy source to work more effectively with external customers. That's a *win* (family)-*win* (you)-*win* (team members)-*win* (external customers) situation!

Imagine for just a moment the synergy that can be created everywhere if all of us live by Boswell's simple rule.

– 96 –

Do what you said you were going to do, when you said you were going to do it, and how you said you were going to do it.

– 97 –
One more thing

This book is finished, but you're not through. Learning, changing, and maximizing your potential to become the best version of you is a lifelong process. Life is a personal development course, and every day is rich with learning opportunities. You want to capitalize upon the opportunities, as you want your sales career to improve your quality of life. Yes, financial success can improve the quality of life for you and your family, but we're talking about much more than that. Consider for the moment the many topics we've discussed that can have a positive impact upon you and your family. We're going to recap and list a few of the critical ones. (We could list additional life-changing competencies that we've discussed, but the format of this book makes it easy for you to quickly review chapters that are important to you.)

1. Optimism

Research shows that optimistic people live healthier and longer lives. In addition, optimistic people certainly live happier lives because of their focus on the good.

2. Resilience

You're going to experience disappointment and frustration in every aspect of your life. The faster you learn to bounce back, the faster you can get on with living the more positive elements of life.

3. Self-confidence

The more you learn about self-confidence, the easier it is to teach your children how to achieve the self-confidence that is essential for their careers and quality of life. You want to pass it on.

4. Self-esteem

Self-esteem is another personal characteristic that touches every component of your life. As with self-confidence, you learn it. You want to help others to do the same.

We hope that after reading this book, you're more encouraged to be a serious student who enthusiastically embraces this lifelong process of taking your sales career to the next level. There are many excellent learning resources. For example, Jim Cathcart authored an excellent book, *Relationship Selling: The Eight Competencies of Top Sales Producers,* based on the premise of selling differently to different people. Lorna Riley has one of the more comprehensive learning and accountability systems we've had the opportunity to review. You can check it out by logging onto www.lornariley.com. She is also the author of *76 Ways to Build a Straight Referral Business, ASAP.* Paul Vitale loaded his book, *Sell with Confidence: Unlock Your Potential,* with very useful content. And Steven Gaffney and Colleen Francis wrote *Honesty Sells: How to Make More Money and Increase Business Profits.*

Conclusion

As in the introduction, we would like to end this book with a story (author unknown) that depicts the life of a very successful sales professional who was envied by his peers.

And in those days, behold, there came through the gates of the city a salesman from afar off, and it came to pass as the day went by he sold plenty.

And in that city were they that were the order takers and they that spent their days in adding to the alibi sheets. Mightily were they astonished. They said one to the other, "How doth he getteth away with it?" And it came to pass that many were gathered in the back office and a soothsayer came among them. And he was one wise guy. And they spoke and questioned him saying, "How is it that this stranger accomplisheth the impossible?"

Whereupon the soothsayer made answer: "He of whom you speak is one hustler. He ariseth very early in the morning and goeth forth full of pep. He complaineth not, neither doth he know despair. He is arrayed in purple and fine linen, while ye go forth with pants unpressed.

"While ye gather here and say one to the other, 'Verily this is a terrible day to work,' he is already abroad. And when the eleventh hour cometh, he needeth no alibis. He knoweth his line and they that would stave him off, they give him orders. Men say unto him 'nay' when he cometh in, yet when he goeth forth he hath their names on the line that is dotted.

"He taketh with him the two angels 'inspiration' and 'perspiration' and worketh to beat hell. Verily I say unto you, go and do likewise.

As we leave you, we're asking you to put this book in an accessible place so you can quickly review a quote or chapter that will provide the needed psychological boost to keep you at your peak performance throughout the day. Additionally, from the list of new behaviors that you've discovered—those essential to taking your sales career to the next level—we recommend that you implement the 2/24/90 Principle™ by identifying the two most important behaviors within the next twenty-four hours and work on improving them for the next ninety days. When you master these, start the process over with two new behaviors. We would also like to share two more disciplines found in what we call the Rule of Ten™ that, when implemented, will help you achieve your goals.

First, we recommend that you read ten pages a day from a self-improvement book—that's a three-hundred-page book a month! We've referenced several winners in the previous pages. We also highly recommend *The Greatest Salesman in the World* by Og Mandino, *How I Raised Myself from Failure to Success in Selling* by Frank Bettger, and David Allen's books, *Getting Things Done: The Art of*

Stress-Free Productivity and *Ready for Anything: 52 Productivity Principles for Work and Life.* Pick one and start reading!

Second, since the number one want of your clients is to be appreciated, start sending ten handwritten notes per week (that's only two per day) thanking them for their business and friendship. Once you start practicing the 2/24/90 Principle and the Rule of Ten, you'll be amazed at the positive impact these simple acts of daily discipline will have on your life and your sales career.

Finally, we leave you with the following words:
Work hard
Do your best
Live the truth
Trust yourself
Have some fun
. . . and you'll have no regrets!

May your life and sales career always be green and growing.

Your friends on the journey to significance,

Byrd Baggett

Larry Cole

Check out these other books in the  *series:*